THE SUN IMAGES

by the same Author

in English

Vishnudharmottara Purana, Vol. I & II, G.O. Series, Baroda
Tilaka (Hindu Marks on the forehead)
Shree Vishnudharmottara (A text on ancient Indian arts)
Pauranic Ritualism
Descriptive Catalogue of Sanskrit Manuscripts, Vol. I & II

in Sanskrit (the critical editions of)

Krishnagiti of Somanatha
Śṛangāra hārāvali of Shri Harṣa
Vasturatnakośa
Nṛtta Saṅgraha
Nṛtyādhyāya of Aśoka Malla
Nṛtyaratnakośa of Śri kumbhakarṇa, Vol. I & II
Pramānamanjari
Mudrā vicāra prakaraṇam

in Gujarati

Ancient Indian Architecture and Sculpture
Hindu Iconography
Jain Iconography
Tibet
Patthara Bole chhe
Shree and Sanskriti
Indian Archaeology (translation)

THE SUN IMAGES

PRIYABALA SHAH

ADITYA PRAKASHAN
NEW DELHI

First published 1996

₹450/.00

ISBN 81-86471-07-3

Published by Pradeep Kumar Goel for Aditya Prakashan,
F-14/65 Model Town II, Delhi–110 009 and printed at
D.K. Fine Art Press, C-2/9, Community Centre,
Ashok Vihar Phase II, Delhi - 110 052

CONTENTS

Preface vii

List of Plates ix

Abbreviations x

Prayer (For Sun-God) xi

CHAPTER

1. Evidences of Images in the early Sanskrit Literature 1
2. Sūrya: The Names and the Cult 16
3. Description of the Sun Images in Sanskrit Literature 27
4. Description of the Images of Sūrya 49
5. Comparisons and Conclusions 94

APPENDIX

1. Images in Tabular Form 108
2. Inscriptions 123
3. Sun Temples and Images (Gujarat) 129

Bibliography 131

Index 135

Plates 142

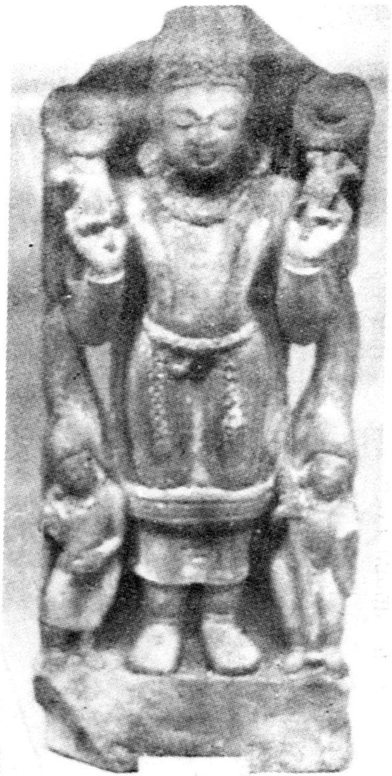

British Museum

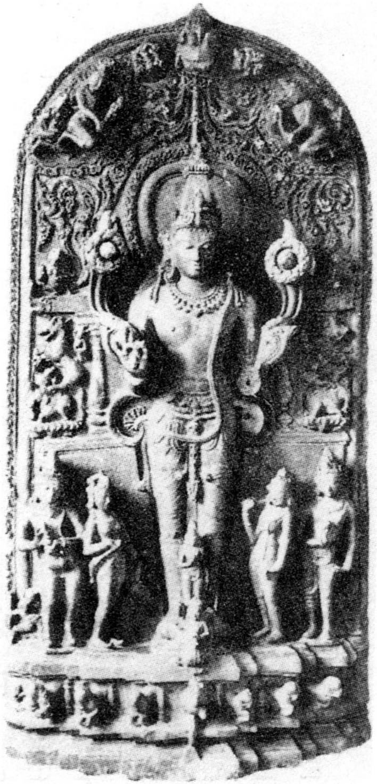

Rājshāhi Museum

Sūrya, Northern and Southern style

PREFACE

The Sun-God who was popular in the Vedic age continued to be worshipped even in the post Vedic period. The cult of Sun is said to have been imported by Sāmba from the Śakadvipa. The epics and the Purāṇas including Mahātmyas contain many references to the spread of the Sun-cult in Gujarat as well as in North and South India.

The old inscriptions allude to a number of Sun-temples, the period of which ranges from the fifth century A.D. onwards. The archaeological remains of the old temples and icons of the Sun-God fully corroborate the data supplied by the literary and epigraphic sources.

The Sun (Sūrya) is a gem of the sky. He shines for all the world. He dispels the darkness with his light. He is the symbol of the light, heat and fertility. He presents himself to his worshippers with three chief aspects which are the rising, culminating and setting Sun. These are not separated or distinguished as three deities but are varying forms of one and the same God, in each of which he displays himself with different attributes and as exercising different powers. By his power he drives away the demons of sickness and expels diseases.

Yet the solar cult of India has not received its due attention as is given to other cults.

In later literature Sūrya and nine planets (Nava-graha) are iconographically represented and made the object of a cult. The cult of the Sun which is the most important is closely connected with that of Viṣṇu, who is identified with the Sun in the Vedas. The special worship of Sūrya is well-known to Vedic and Iranian sources.

In the completion of the present work, I have been helped by many in more ways than one and my acknowledgements are due to all. I am extremely grateful to Dr. (Prof.) R.N. Mehta, a well known archaeologist. He has been very kind to me in going through the manuscript and suggesting to me many ideas regarding the arrangement of material before it was sent to press.

Here I take the opportunity to express my deep sense of gratitude and indebtedness to my research teacher, Prof. R.C. Parikh, the then Director of B.J. Institute of Learning and Research, Ahmedabad for the very great interest which he envinced in the present work.

In this work, I have relied upon the works of learned scholars in the field of research, particularly Burgess, Fergusson, Cousens, Cunningham, Coomaraswamy, Bhandarkar and others, and also on some of the bulletins of the different museums of archaeology. I acknowledge my debt to them as by their courtsey. I have reproduced some of the photographs herein.

I cannot end this preface before expressing my sense of gratitude to Shree Pradeep Kumar Goel of Aditya Prakashan, Delhi, whose keen interest in this work has made possible the prompt publication of this work.

Mahashivaratri
17 February 1996

Priyabala Shah
"Jeevan-Kala"
12, Sadma Society,
Ahmedabad – 380 009

A LIST OF PLATES

	Description on page
Frontispiece	
Sūrya in British Museum	
Sūrya in Rājashāhi Museum	
1. Sūrya – Bodhagaya Railing	53
2. Sūrya – Bhājā	53
3. Sūrya – Mathura	54
4. Sūrya (Kuṣāṇa) – Mathurā	54
5. Sūrya (Black Stone) – Gāndhāra	54
6. Sūrya – Garhwa (Allahabad)	55
7. Sūrya – Ellorā	55
8. Sūrya – Guḍimallam	58
9. Sūrya – Moḍhera	63
10. Sūrya – Moḍhera	63
11. Sūrya – Sarkhej (Ahmedabad)	67
12. Sūrya – Konarka	70
13. Sūrya – Khair Khaneh	77

ABBREVIATIONS

A G	Āśvalāyana Gṛhyasūtra
A.S.I.	Archaeological Survey of India
A V	Atharvaveda
B G	Bhagavadgītā
C A I	Coins of Ancient India
D.H.I.	Development of Hindu Iconography
E H I	Elements of Hindu Iconography
K U S	Kumāra Sambhava
M B H	Mahābhārata
N S	Nāṭyaśāstra
J A O S	Journal of American Oriental Society
J R A S	Journal of Royal Asiatic Society
R V	Rigveda
V D	Viṣṇudharmottara

Prayer (for Sun-God)

"O thou, whose manifestation is the universe, thou art the abode of auspicious splendours, be pleased. O glorious one and put in me (endow me with) the resources of a leader in a pre-eminent degree. O Lord of the world, destroy whatever sin I, humble that I am, might have committed. O divine one, Vouch safe to me every kind of blessing for the attainment of supreme good."

Kalyāṇānām tvamasi mahasām
Bhājanam Viśvamūrte
Dhūryām ḷakṣmī matha mahī
dhehi deva prasīda/
Yad yad pāpam pratijahi
jagannātha namrasya tanme
Bhadram Bhadram (bhūyo bhūyo) vitaran Bhagavan
bhūyase mangalāya///
(Mālatī Mādhava, Act I, Verse 3)

ONE

EVIDENCES OF IMAGES IN THE EARLY SANSKRIT LITERATURE

In view of the fact that other ancient countries, such as Greece, had images in the 800 BC and Egypt had, of course, at a still older date, one is led to suspect whether India has, if not greater, similar claims to antiquity of her images, being universally pronounced as an idolatrous country. The beginnings of sculptures in India can be traced back to a very remote age. Harappan art of about the third millennium BC shows a high state of proficiency which suggests a much earlier development. Indian prehistory is slowly pushing this limit backwards. Prior to these discoveries, it was vehemently argued that iconographic development in India began late, and interesting arguments were advanced to support this hypothesis. These authors argued that the belief that image making was known in India in the Vedic Age[1], is unjustified. Grünwedel remarks in the introduction to his well-known essay on "Buddhist Art", that "the art of Ancient India owes its rise to Buddhism," and he, as well as other authorities, lay stress on the fact that it is essentially ornamental. Foucher[2] says "the Ancient Indian sculpture did not know detached statues...." It is a well-known fact that the later Indian school counts only a few ones, which have not been placed against a wall or a pillar. The reason is that "sculpture was considered as a purely ornamental art." Grünwedel has also shown, how wood-carving and the goldsmith's craft have existed in India from the ancient time and paved the way for an Indian school of sculpture. The oldest Indian sculpture known up to the present time, is found in old Buddhist monuments. The Buddha himself is not, however, represented. It is only when a new school of art had been started under the influence of *Greek artists on the north-western* frontier,

---

[1] The Development of Early Hindu Iconography by S.V. Venkateśwara in *JRAS*, 1917, p. 587.

[2] *Revue de l' Histoire des Religions*, Vol. 30, 1894, p. 337.

that we come to know about the statues of the founder of the religion. Sten Konow,[3] controverting the theories of those, whose opinion it was that Indian art began after the Buddhist age, touched the problem and remarked, it would, however, be unwise to infer that the Indians learnt to worship images from the Greeks, or that the practice of adoring images of the Buddha was inaugurated by the semi-Greek population of the Punjab, as maintained by Fergusson and Cunningham[4]. It is not intended to take up the question, where and when the practice of making images of the Buddha was first started. The intention is only to remind a few facts, which show that the Indians had been making images, even before the rise of the Buddhist (art of the) Gāndhāra school.

"In the pre-Buddhistic phase of Indian religion from which Hinduism is directly descended, carved images of the gods and temples for worship were equally unknown. It is hardly to be expected that the very rudimentary art of that early age should have attempted to represent in an anthropomorphic form of gods which were still felt to be the deifications of forces of natural phenomena, such as sun, fire, sky, wind and in the absence of images, structural places of worship would not be wanted."[5] I do not, however, think that this characterisation applies to the time immediately preceding the rise of Buddhism. On the contrary, it is a well-known fact that we find representations of Hindu gods on Buddhist monuments from a pre-Gāndhāra school. It is, for the present, sufficient to mention the representations of the Goddess Śrī in Udayagiri, Bharhut and Sanchi. The stereotype way, in which she is represented everywhere, points back to a long development, and shows that there is no real objection against the theory, that there existed images of Hindu gods at a comparatively early period.

We shall deal, at length, with the literary and other evidences which go to prove the existence of Indian images and their worship

---

[3] Notes on the use of images in Ancient India, *Indian Antiquary,* 1909, p. 145.
[4] See Foucher, *Beginnings of Buddhist Art*, London, 1918, p. 326.
[5] *JRAS*, Vol. LVII, 1909, p. 317.

at a much earlier time than is commonly supposed. It is sufficient to say at present that the time would coincide with the time of the personification of gods by the Vedic Rishis. Archaeological research slowly and steadily brings out evidences of smaller images of different deities, that were made in India.

The origin of image worship in India, appears to be very ancient, yet, its causes are not exactly known. Many believe that it may be the result of the followers of Gautam Buddha, who were adoring their master and worshipping in the form of images on his apotheosis after death. However, there are indications of the prevalence of image worship, among the Hindus long before the time of Gautam Buddha, as one can see in Mohen-jo-daro and Harappa.

The symbols were worshipped during the period of Indus Valley culture. As the worship of the sun by means of symbols continued during the subsequent periods and several of them are found described in the Vedic literature and marked on potteries and punch marked coins, it can reasonably be assumed that the pre-Vedic symbols were probably their forerunners. The employment of an external object, to concentrate the mind in the act of meditation in carrying on the practice of Yoga, is as old as the Yoga of Upaniṣads and Patañjali. Patañjali codified the known information. Buddha, as can be seen in his sculptured representations of the Gāndhāra school, is represented as an emaciated person almost dying under the stress of the austerities he practised.[6]

The most critical scholars now do not hesitate in believing that from the pre-Buddhist times — the sūtras of Pāṇini, the Brāhmaṇas of the different Vedas etc. made distinct references to images of gods, which had a history and growth from a time much earlier than the times of the works just mentioned. We shall show here, that the sūtra literature makes mention of such images, as the ingenuity of scholastic criticism.

This definitely brings the age of iconology in India, close to the time of the Vedas. We shall next show that the Vedas consisting

[6] Agrawal, V.S., *Sculptures in the Curzon Museum of Archaeology*, Fig. 43.

of the Saṁhitās and the Brāhmaṇas give sufficient evidences for the knowledge and the use of images in that age. Descriptions of the Vedic gods and goddesses as having hands, feet, armours, dresses, chariots, vehicles are in reality, the progenitors of the descriptions of images such as we find in the early Purāṇas and the Śilpaśāstras. It is admitted also that, in later ages, the images of gods were multiplied with variations in their conceptions, in a long evolution of images that appear to run through the different ages of Indian religious life.

We quote here, some of the passages regarding the evidences of the images, from the early Sanskrit literature.

THE VEDIC SAṀHITĀS

That the Vedas, should contain sculptural directions and devices, would be rather too illogical to expect as those early hymns of mankind, were not meant specifically to represent a Śilpaśāstra or a science of art. So far as images or sculptures are concerned, our legitimate expectation ought to be to find anthropomorphic descriptions of gods and goddesses with details of limbs, dresses, arms, armours, vehicles and so on.

And these we find in the Saṁhitās in plenty. The Vedas are not strictly a practical code of Dharma, and thus we can scarcely get there such things as consecration or installation of sacred objects. For these, we may have to look for books specially devoted to them. And the books of the Vedic affiliation of this branch of literature give abundant references to image and image-worship.

In the Vedas themselves, we may come across here and there hints of an image or passages, which convey, as a whole, the sure indication of an image, and probably that may be practically enough for a historic and inferential scrutiny. We discuss here some of these passages —

The Vājasaneyī Saṁhitā of the White Yajurveda has a number of references to the subject of images, which cannot be constructed otherwise. In one passage, the Sun-God has been called Hiraṇya-pāṇi or "One whose hands are made of gold". This also alludes to the fact that the hands of the Sun-God (no doubt of his image) once broken by the iconoclasm of the demons, were replaced by a pair of golden arms by the gods.[7] There are other passages in the same Saṁhitā which clearly indicate the existence of images in the Vedic age. As for example, 'the body of Agni made of Ayas or of silver or of gold,'[8] 'Agni being carried by the bearers',[9] 'the presiding deities of night and dawn having fine sculptures',[10] 'the wood-engraver who makes image,' etc.[11] The *Taittirīya Saṁhitā* of the Black Yajurveda-school gives evidence to the use of image in sacrifice in a passage, such as "He puts down a golden man, to support the world of the sacrifice"[12]; "This is the temple of gods," etc.[13] Similarly, the word Devala meaning 'One who earns by dealing with images' has been mentioned as a Ṛṣi in the Kāṭhaka Saṁhitā.[14] The Atharvaveda Saṁhitā refers to the setting up of a sanctuary.[15] The Sāmaveda has this passage for an image, which is plain enough — "We approach the foe-destroying, ancient incarnate Agni, who shone forth most illustriously in the form of Śrutavana, the son of Arksha."[16]

The passages we quote below should be discussed relatively, so that we may understand by their comparative and co-relative implications, whether the Vedic Indians were familiar with the use of images, such extracts are:

"Varuṇa, wearing golden mail, hath clad him in a shining robe. His spies are seated about[17] of many forms, mighty, of tawny colour, he is painted with limbs solid, bright and golden. From Rudra the great lord of this world may power never be

---

[7] Devo vaḥ Savitā Hiraṇyapāṇiḥ pratigṛabhṇātvacchidreṇa pāṇinā/ Ad. 1-15 K-16, Vājasaneyī Saṁhitā.

[8] Ibid., Ad. V-8.

[9] Ibid., X. 26.

[10] Suśilpe Yadvai Pratirūpam tacchilpamiti Śruteḥ Suṣṭhu Śilpam X. 28-29, commentary.

[11] Ibid., 30, 12.

[12] Keith's Veda of the Black Yajurveda, Vol.II, p. 411, footnote, p. 320.

[13] Taittirīya Saṁhitā (Tukaram, Bombay), p. 53.

[14] Macdonell and Keith's *Vedic Index*.

[15] The Atharvaveda II, ii, 2, iv-40-1; viii, 5, 1, 4.

[16] Sāmaveda, i, 9, 5; 7, 9.

[17] Rv. I-25-13 (from *Indian Images* by Bhattacharya).

taken away.[18] May (the gods) waited upon by the hymn come to the seven worlds of the invoker, and delight the world with the holy water. May the numerous doors of human form, born in the sacrifices, come to this sacrifice.[19] The two kings that never do evil, sit in the highest place (that is) firm (and is) supported on a thousand pillars."[20]

Kaegi gives the following translation:

"Who offers me ten cows for this Indra of mine? When he has overcome the enemy he will return to me... recalling. Not even for a high price would I exchange thee, thou that art armed with sling-stones, not for thousands, not for myriads (of cows), not for a hundred-fold price, thou with hundred fold riches".[21]

At the end, one can say that the forms of the deities were at first comparatively few and simple; afterwards, partly by the recognition of new divinities of popular origin, partly by the deification of metaphysical concepts, the number of aspects and variety of forms increased. It may be remarked that after the first century AD the typical form of a god is four-armed. The additional arms are to carry the attributes of the god: still more complicated forms have come into use at later periods.[22] Finally, it may be said that the visible imagery of the Hindu (and Buddhist) pantheon represents as precisely as the written texts, an encyclopedia of Indian psychological and social, ethical and physical science — each divinity or aspect of divinity (for all are referred to one source) representing a particular power or force or combination of forces. "The purpose of the innovation was the practical one of supplying a means of displaying the symbols without which the gods could not be adequately identified when represented by themselves apart from the adjunct of a *Vāhana*.." One of the latest concepts to be deified after this fashion is that of

---

18 Rv. II-33-9 (from *Indian Images* by Bhattacharya).

19 Rv. III-4-5 (from *Vedārtha Yatna* by S.P. Pandit).

20 Rv. II-41-45 (from *Vedārtha Yatna* by S.P. Pandit).

21 ".... is hardly conceivable without an image or some symbol of the gods" (see Kaegi, RV. note 79).

22 See Macdonell, *JRAS*, pp. 125-130 and also A.K..Coomaraswamy, *Museum of Fine Arts* (Boston).

Motherland, the Bhārata Mātā of Indian Nationalism. However, this trend continues in the deity like Santoshi Mā and others. The fruit of the worship of such deities results from the effects of the worshipper's own spiritual acts upon his own personality and is very far from unreal.[23]

THE BRĀHMAṆAS AND ĀRAṆYAKAS[24]

Informations with respect to the prevalence of images are sufficiently contained in this branch of the Vedic literature. In the Ṣaḍviṁśa Brāhmaṇa, we read "The temples of Gods tremble, the images of Gods laugh, cry, dance, break etc."[25] The expression, Deva-malimuca meaning 'a robber of the Gods' being the epithet of Rahasya as used in the Pañca-Viṁśa Brāhmaṇa shows clear indication of images in the context of that Brāhmaṇa.[26] The Śatapatha Brāhmaṇa gives directions for making a gold image of a Puruṣa placed on the image of the sun with rays all made of gold which again has been placed upon the petals of a lotus.[27] In the same Brāhmaṇa references have been made to the images of Rātrī (The Goddess of night), Kāladeva (The God of time) and others to be engraved on bricks.[28]

Similarly, such passages as "To sleep by a God in a Gārhapatyāgāra", "Gods being adorned with a holy thread", "Śiva with Pināka attired in a tiger's skin", "She sacrifices sitting in front of the Gods",[29] etc. allude to images by the meaning of the word Deva etc. They require little explanation or commentary. The Sānkhyāyana Brāhmaṇa of the Rigveda contains several stray references to images. The passages, for instance, "He

---

[23] Coomaraswamy A.K., Museum of Fine Arts, Boston.

[24] *The Vedic Literature* (last phase): c. 1500 BC–2000 BC (Whitney, Hall and Macdonell). 4500 BC (Jacobi, Tilak).

[25] Sa Param diva... devatāyatanāni, Kampante Daivatapratimā hasanti rudanti Nṛtyanti, Sphuṭanti Khidyanti Unmilanti — Sāmaveda, Ṣaḍviṁsa Brāhmaṇa — V-10.

[26] Pañca-Viṁśa Brāhmaṇa, XXIII, 18, 1. The same expression occurs in the same meaning in Tāṇḍya Brāhmaṇa, XIV, 4.

[27] Ibid., IV-8-18.

[28] Ibid., X-3, 13-19, 220.

[29] Ibid., (Bibli Indica), Vol.I, p. 8, Vol.II, pp. 190, 389, Vol.III, p. 9.

addresses and cleans Ilā", "The arms of the Sun- God being broken, they gave two golden arms" and so on are significant enough.[30] Several passages connected with images occur in the Taittirīya Brāhmaṇa of the Black Yajurveda, some of which are mentioned here: "The Udgātā having laid in front of the Gods,"[31] "Agni is on the Chariot",[32] "Those Gods are in the Chariots,"[33] "Let the hotā worship the two images of Uṣā",[34] The three images of Saraswatī, Iḍā and Bhārati",[35] "The two images of the presiding deities of day and night",[36] "The three Goddesses made of Gold",[37] "Tvaṣṭā the sculptor of various images",[38] "All these devatās are for the merit of the Yajamāna put on the Chariot".[39] The Vedic Āraṇyakas are no less replete with allusions to images. The Aitareya-Āraṇyaka contains a few of these, such as "I have constructed the body of the God Indra".[40]

Clear evidences of images may be seen in the Taittirīya Āraṇyaka, some of which are mentioned here: The clothes of deities used to be dyed yellow,[41] the Rudras had their white clothes,[42] the seven suns represented in the art of Kaśyapa,[43] "Let Viśvakarmā provide you with sun-images", "Let Tvaṣṭā provide

[30] Yadilāmupahvayate Yanmārjate/ (p. 11) Pāṇī Praticcheda tasmai Hiraṇmayau Pratidadhustasmātdhiraṇyapāṇiriti (p. 21) Sāmkhyāyana Brāhmaṇa (Anandasrama Sanskrit Series) p. 64.

[31] The Taittirīya Brāhmaṇa (Anandasrama Sanskrit Series) p. 108.

[32] Ibid., p. 133.

[33] Yā eva devatā rathe praviṣṭaḥ//.... same page.

[34] Ibid., p. 635.

[35] Ibid., p. 641.

[36] Ibid., p. 654.

[37] Ibid., p. 681.

[38] Ibid., p. 1194.

[39] Ibid., p. 1249.

[40] Indrasya tanu Śariram parito Nirmitavānasmi iti Sāyaṇa slaoh (Anandasrama Skt. Series) pp. 142-43

[41] Devatānām Vastrāṇi Ca Śṛngārārtham Haridrādi dravyaranjitāni bhavanti/ Taittirīya-Āraṇyaka, edited by Rajendralal Mitra, p. 20.

[42] Ibid., p. 22.

[43] Yatte Śilpam Kaśyapa Rocanāvat/...Yasmin Suryā arpitāḥ Saptasākam/ p. 80. This reference may be regarded as very important from the point of sculptural art as it refers so early to the art of Kaśyapa whose work known as Kaśyapa śilpa-śāstra though not in its earliest version has yet been handed down to us.

you with images",[44] "The learned Tvaṣṭā the maker of images",[45] "Thou art an image".[46] In Vedic sacrifices certain bricks formed a chief material and there is good ground for believing that the sacrificial bricks used to bear reliefs of figures like sacrificial posts. The Taittirīya Āraṇyaka contains some topics concerning these bricks.

THE SŪTRA LITERATURE[47]

Both the Gṛhya Sūtras and the Śrauta Sūtras make clear reference to the existence of images of gods. The installation of an image, a temple of an image has been mentioned, go to prove that image worship was sufficiently common in those times.[48]

A number of references to an image may be gathered from Bodhāyana Gṛhya Sūtra which presents a variety of gods as worshipped during the author's time. He deals at length with the rituals of bath, purification, daily worship, etc. connected with the installation of an image in these connections, the images of Viṣṇu, Mahāpuruṣa, Vināyaka or Gaṇeśa, Yama have been referred to in the book.[49] The author always refers to gold images as were presumably prevalent in his time. The village gods have also been mentioned in the book. The Kauśika Sūtra of the

---

[44] Ibid., p. 126. It is also worthy of remark that Viśvakarmā and Tvaṣṭā were two divine artists.

[45] Ibid., p. 308.

[46] *Pratimā Asi*, p. 425.

[47] The Sūtra period — pre-Pāṇinian. The date of Manu given as 200 BC by the scholars is not convincing. He certainly preceded the other law givers in date. As the last redaction made was not later than 200 BC (Bühler), the original Sūtras may be reasonably assigned to this period.

[48] Devakulam — a temple, Śāmkhyāyana Gṛhya Sūtra.

[49] Athāto Viṣṇupratiṣṭhākalpam Vyākhyāsyāmaḥ...
Suvarṇopadhānam pratikṛtim /p. 238.
Athāto Mahāpuruṣasyāharaḥ paricaryā Vidhim Vyākhyāsyāmaḥ.... devasya pratikṛtim Kṛtvā /p. 243.
Athāto Rudrapratiṣṭhā Kalpam Vyākhyāsyāmaḥ /p. 247.
Athāto Durgākalpaṁ Vyākhyāsyāmaḥ /p. 269.
Athātaḥ Śrīkalpam Vyākhyāsyāmaḥ /p. 271.
Athāto Ravikalpam Vyākhyāsyāmaḥ /p. 276.
Athāto Vināyakakalpam Vyākhyāsyāmaḥ /p. 278.
Athāto Yamakalpam Vyākhyāsyāmaḥ /p. 285.
The Bodhāyana Gṛhya Sūtra (Govt. Oriental Library Series, Mysore).

Atharvaveda repeatedly refers to the fact that the gods were dancing, falling, laughing and singing. Traces of the belief of houses, villages, towns, fields and temple by Gods being haunted are to be found in this ancient work and their remedial measures are also given.[50] The Āśvalāyana Gṛhyasūtra furnishes, in the like manner, unequivocal evidences of image worship. The household and guardian deities have been specifically mentioned.[51]

In this Gṛhya Pariśiṣṭa of the same book may be found topics related to images of the planets, the materials to be used for their construction and so on.[52]

MANU AND OTHER SMĀRTA BOOKS[53]

In the laws of Manu may be found several references to images. One of the duties of a Brahmacārī was to worship an image of God.[54] Mention has been made of a Devalaka or a Brahmin of inferior order who subsists upon the offerings made to the images which he attends.[55]

Manu contains rules about circumambulating an image, stepping on its shadow and refers to the taking of oaths in its presence.[56] He also gives ordinances to be observed in dealing with a

---

[50] Daivateṣu nṛtyatṣu cyotatṣu Hasatsu Gāyatsu. The Kauśika Sūtra of the Atharvaveda, edited by M. Bloomfield, p. 246, for repeatition of the same p. 258. Gṛhe grāme vā pattane kṣetre vā devagṛhe vā yatra kvacit piśācaśaniskāsti .... Av. IV Kaṇḍikā, 25, see also the commentary, p. 324.

[51] Etābhyaścaiva devatābhyobhdabhya Oṣadhivanaspatibhyo gṛhāya gṛhadevatā bhyo vāstudevatābhyaḥ./ Āśvālāyana gṛhya sūtra (Bibli, Indi.), p. 8.

[52] Athārcanamācāryaḥ...... Grahapratimām Sthāpayitvā "Vāstumūrtim suvarṇena kṛtvā"// p. 333 (ibid p. 291) also atha pratimādravyāṇi muktāphala śilādāruhematāmra rajatakāṁsya mṛtikādini..../", p. 335.

[53] Gautama — 5th or 6th cent. BC — Jolly's *Recht Und Sitte,* pp. 3-7 Bodhāyana, Āpastamba — 4th or 5th cent. BC, ibid.

[54] Devatābhyarccāñancaiva Samidādhānameva Ca/Manu II, 176. Household gods have been mentioned Cf. ibid., III, 117.

[55] Cikitsakān devalakānmānsavikrayiṇastathā/ibid, III, 152.

[56] Mṛdanga daivatam Vipram... Pradakṣiṇāni Kurvīta Prajñātañśca vanaspatin/ IV, 39 Devatānām Gurorājñaḥ Snātakācārya-Yosthā/ Nākrāmet Kāmataśchhāyām Babhruṇo-dikṣitasya Ca// IV, 30. Devabrāhmaṇasānnidhye Ṣākṣyam pṛcchedṛtam dvijān/ Udam-mukhān Prānmukhānvā pūrvvāhne vai Śuciḥ Śūcin// VIII, 87.

conquered land and one of these refers to the worship of images.[57] In Manu's time among other things, a temple of a god was used to mark a boundary between two lands.[58] Similarly, at that time, iconoclasm was regarded as a penal offence.[59] The Gautama Dharmasūtra, a smārta book of great authority, has some passages bearing on images, e.g. "Looking towards... images of gods, etc. one must not commit nuisance,"[60] "One should circumambulate a temple of gods", etc.,[61] "One who bears on his body sandal and saffron touched by a śālagrama attains salvation",[62] "In a holy place, in a Tīrtha, in the presence of a god," etc.,[63] Then, entering a house of God..."[64] Household gods have also been spoken of in the same religious code.[65] Āpastamba Dharmasūtra, another book on Smṛti furnishes similar evidences of image-worship. Such evidences may be clearly seen in passages, where the author distinguishes the merit of worship from the merit of meditation, etc.[66] in which prohibition against a nuisance committed by one facing a god has been enjoined[67] and where one is forbidden to spread one's feet in the direction of Agni, Brāhmin, God, etc.[68]

THE EPICS

The Mahābhārata is well stocked with references of images.

---

[57] Jitvā sampūjayedevān brāhmaṇānścaiva dhārmikān/ VII, 201.

[58] Taḍāgānyudapānāni Vāpyaḥ Prasravaṇāni Ca/ Sīmāsandhiṣu Kāryāṇi devatāyatanāni Ca// Manu, VIII, 248.

[59] Saṁkramadhvajaṣaṣṭhīṇām Pratimānāśca bhedakaḥ/ IX, 285.

[60] Na.... devatāgāśca pratipaśyanvā mūtrapurīṣāmedhyāni Vyudasyet/ p. 139, p. 458, Gautama-Dharmashastra (Govt. Oriental Library Series, Mysore).

[61] Praśastamaṅgalyadevāyatanacatuṣpathādīn pradakṣiṇamāVarteta// ibid., p. 154.

[62] Śālagrāmaśilā lagnam Kumkumacandanam Vastu dehedhārayate Sa mukto bhavati/ Ibid., p. 465.

[63] Śuddhakṣetratīrtheṣu devatāsannidhau/ ibid., p. 467.

[64] Tato devagṛham Gatvā... Pūjāsambhāra... p. 469.

[65] Gṛhadevatābhyaḥ Praviśya// p. 95.

[66] Samādhi Viśeṣacchrutiviśeṣācca Pūjāyām balaviśeṣaḥ/ Apastamba Dharma (Mysore edition), p. 186.

[67] Brāhmaṇagā devatāścābhimukho Mūtrapurīṣayoḥ Karmavarjayet// ibid., p. 199.

[68] Agnimāpo bhrāhmaṇagā devatā... nābhiprasārayanti// ibid., p. 200.

Several chapters (adhyāyas) are devoted to topics of pilgrimages to holy places.[69] The images of Mahākāla, Śankhakarṇeśvara, Bhīmā, Triśūlapāṇi, Kāmākhyā, Vāmana, Āditya, Saraswatī, Dhūmāvatī, Bhadrakarṇeśvara, Kālikā, Candra and others have been mentioned.[70] The locales of these, as mentioned in the great Epics,[71] seem to be so ancient that it is not at all easy now to identify them. In another chapter we meet with identical references to images.[72] The readers of the Mahābhārata are well aware of the portrait statues (made of iron) of Bhīma[73] and of Droṇācārya as adored by his silent devotee Ekalavya. Similarly the Rāmāyana also mentions many images of which references here seem to be rather redundant.[74]

PATANJALI'S MAHĀBHAṢYA (2ND CENT. BC)

The commentator of Pāṇini Sūtras, in connection with an aphorism gives examples — Vāsudeva, Śiva, Skanda, Viṣṇu and Āditya — which words are here used in the sense of images (Archā) of those gods.[75] The aphorism runs "Jivikārthe Cāpaṇye" (V-3-99), "Apaṇye ityucyate tatredam na siddhyati". It means, a means of livelihood (it being presumed that no traffic is driven thereby).

---

[69] Koṭitirthamupāspṛśya hayamedhaphalam labhet/ MBH (Vanaparva Ad. 82, S10.48–49).

[70] MBH, Vanaparva, Ad. 82-84.

[71] Pre-Buddhistic — the original part of the Rāmāyana composed before 500 BC — Macdonell, Imp. Gaz., Vol.II, p. 237. The old form of the epic probably came into being about the 5th cent. BC, ibid., p. 235.

[72] Devatāpratimāścaiva Prakampante Hasanti ca/ Vamanti Rudhirancānyaiḥ svidyanti prapatanti ca// - Bhīṣma parva Ad. 2, S10.26. Also Pratimāśca likhantyetā saśastrāḥ kāla coditāḥ/ Anyonyamabhidhāvanti śiśavodaṇḍapāṇayaḥ// ibid., Ad. 3, S10.29.

[73] Bhīmamākṣipya pāṇibhyām pradadau Bhīmamāyasam/ MBH, Strīparva, Ad. 12, S10.14-19.

[74] Devatāgāra... The Rāmāyaṇa 2, 4, 29 pratimāśca prakampante/ ibid., 6, 11, 28.

[75] Shivaḥ Skandaḥ Viśākhe iti/ kim karaṇam /Mauryairhiraṇya vārthibhirarcāḥ Prakalpitaḥ/ Bhavettāsu na syāt /yāstvetāḥ samprati pūjārthāstāsu bhaviṣyati/ (The Vyakarana Mahabhasya of Patanjali, edited by F. Keilhorn (B.S.S.) Vol.II, p. 429.

An illustration of another aphorism, the images of Kaśyapa have been mentioned.[76] The same old scholium informs us of the beating and the sounding of the Mṛdanga, Śankha, the existence of a sect of Śivabhāgavatas holding an iron lance in their hands.[77] Thus the representations of the principal gods of the Indian pantheon were no less common in those days than they are now. In another passage of the Mahābhāṣya, the author in explanation of the aphorism of Pāṇini (IV-1-54), gives examples of an image having a large nose or a high nose.[78] This is a direct proof that Pāṇini knew of statues and images of gods.

The aphorism of Pāṇini[79]: Pāṇini in his Aṣṭādhyāyī explains the termination 'ka' in the sense of similarity or likeness. He says "Ive Pratikṛtau". There is a commentary (kāśikāvṛtti) on it, which explains this sūtra as 'Kan'... Ivārthaḥ, Sādṛaśyam, tasya viśeṣaṇam pratikṛtigrahaṇam.

Apart from the references given in Patañjali's *Mahābhāṣya*, the Sūtras themselves contain a passage which pertains to the subject of an image. According to the aphorism the affix *Kan* means a "Likeness", when the imitation of a thing is to be expressed. Thus Aśva ivāyamaśva pratikṛtiḥ aśvakaḥ — an imitation of a horse (in wood or clay, etc.).[80] Again in (V-3-100), he sums up the instances in which the suffix *Kan* is elided as follows:

Arcakāsu Pūjanārthāsu Citrakarmadhvajeṣu Ca/
Ivā Pratikṛtā lopam kano devapathādiṣu//

The affix *Kan* denoting a likeness when the imitation of a thing is to be expressed, is elided when the imitation is (1) an image for worship; (2) a picture; (3) a design on a flag; and (4) the suffix should be added after the gaṇa devapaṭa etc. The

---

[76] Kāśyapapratikṛtayaḥ Kāśyapa iti/ ibid., p. 241.

[77] The point was specially emphasised by R.G. Bhandarkar in his presidential address at the first Oriental Conference (Poona), 1919.

[78] Adravam mūrtimat svaṃgam prāṇisthama vikārajam/ Atatstham tatra dṛṣṭam ca tasya cettattathā yutam/ Dīrghanāsikyarccā.../ Tuṁga nāsikyarceti/ Mahābhāṣyam. Keilhorn, Vol.II, p. 222.

[79] 7th cent. BC, Goldstücker and R.G. Bhandarkar.

[80] Ive pratikṛtau/ Pāṇini's Aṣṭādhyāyī, V-3, 96.

instances of such images are found in Śiva and Viṣṇu and also in pictures Arjuna and Duryodhan. The juxtaposition of Archā (image) and Chitrakarma (picture), shows that the author of the Kārikā thought of real images and not of symbols.

Patañjali's commentary on Pāṇini (V-3-99) has been fully discussed by the Late Prof. Weber[81] and others. Patañjali says: "Āpaṇya ityucyate tatra edam na siddhyati/ Śivaḥ Skandaḥ Viśākha iti kim kāraṇam/ Mauryair hiraṇyā vārthibhir arcāḥ prakalpitaḥ/ bhavet tāsu na syāt/ yāstu etaḥ/ Sampratipūjārthāstāsu bhaviṣyati ". It is said (by Pāṇini) provided that no traffic is driven thereby in such cases the rules do not apply to (images of) Śiva, Skanda and Viśākha. The Mauryas had images made for greed. Well, the rule does not apply to such (images) but to those that for immediate worship (i.e. such images which are made as a means of subsistence by a low order of Brāhmaṇas, not by selling them, but by exhibiting them from door to door). There cannot be the slightest doubt that images of the gods made for the purpose of worship existed at the time of Patañjali and that these images represented gods such as Śiva, Skanda and Viśākha, the god of war. The images which the Mauryas had caused to be made were called Śivaka, Skandaka etc., that is to say, the image was considered as a likeness so long as it was an article for sale. But, the image of Śiva which the priest carried about and allowed to be worshipped for money was no more "an image of Śiva", it was a "Śiva". The fact, that the Mauryas thought of making money out of trade in images, shows that the demand was considerable. All we can conclude is that during Patañjali's times, and most likely also in the days of Pāṇini, images of the Gods were in existence in India.

KAUṬILYA'S ARTHAŚĀSTRA[82]

The common worship of images in ancient India is attested by passages from the *Arthaśāstra*, now a favourite study among

---

[81] *Indische studient*, Vol.V, pp. 147ff.

[82] C. 320 BC — Jolly, *ZDMG*, Vol.67, pp. 49-96, also pp. 95-96. Hillebrandt shares the same view.

the archaeologists. It too makes mention of the principal deities. "In the centre of the city, the apartments of gods such as Aparājita, Apratihata, Jayanta, Vaijayanta, Śiva, Vaiśravaṇa, Aśvin (divine physicians) and the honourable liqour-house (Śrī Madirāgṛham), shall be situated. In the corners of the ground, the guardian deities shall be appropriately set up, likewise, the principal gates-Brāhma, Aindra, Yāmya and Saināpatya shall be constructed... places of worship and pilgrimage groves and buildings shall be constructed. Guardian deities of all quarters shall also be set up in quarters, appropriate to them".[83]

[83] Aparājitāpratihata Jayanta Vaijayanta Koṣṭhakān Śivavaiśravaṇāśvi śrīmadirāgṛham ca puramadhye kārayet/ koṣṭha kāla yeśu Yathoddeśam vāstudevatāḥ Sthāpayt / Brāhmaindrayāmya Saināpatyāni dvārāṇi Vāhi Parimāyaḥ dhanuśśatavākṛṣṭāścaitya Puṇyasthānavanasetubandhāḥ Kāryā/ Yathā dīśam ca Digdevatāḥ/ *Kautilya Arthasastram*, p. 129 edited by Pandit Ganapati Shastri (Trivandrum, 1924). The translation of the honourable liquor house for Sri Madirāgṛham seems to be incorrect and inappropriate here. It should be translated as a house for Saraswatī with Lakṣmī (Śrīmatirāgṛham) Iḍā means both Saraswatī and Pṛthivī.

Two

SURYA: THE NAMES AND THE CULT

The worship of the sun, as a very prominent deity, was prevalent almost all over the ancient world. Vedic India too had a vigorous tradition of sun-worship. It forms an integral part of nature-worship so prominently practised by the Indo-Āryans.[1] No doubt, the worship of the sun is one of the common features of the religious lives of the Indo-Europeans, the Indo-Iranians and the Indo-Āryans. It is indicated by the presence of a common word for the sun in many Āryan languages. Thus, the Egyptians had worshipped the sun under various names such as Horus, Re, etc., the Assyro-Babylonians used to worship a solar deity, named Marduk. The ancient Iranians paid their homage to the Sun-God under the name of Mithra. Helios, Apollo, the Sun-God occupied a very prominent position in the religious pantheon of the ancient Greeks. In fact, the religious history of every nation, if properly investigated, would clearly show that the worship of the sun in some form or other, was an all important part of worship in certain periods of its existence as a nation. The reason is not far to seek: the sun as the celestial luminary appealed foremost to the imagination of the people and its final disappearance on the western horizon in the evening gave rise to various mythological tales among various nations, to account for these phenomena.

The earliest available literature of India as well as Iranian elements give very clear idea about the worship of the sun at several places.

The Āryans of the Vedic age were no exception to the general order of mankind and the sun was held by them in the highest esteem along with other Gods and deities. Sacrifices were offered to the Sun-God in various aspects, which were given different names as Dvādaśādityas — each personifying to a greater or lesser extent the different attributes of the sun. The worship of these along with that of Navagrahas came to hold a very impor-

[1] Macdonell, *Vedic Mythology*, p. 2.

tant and unique place in the Brahmanical rituals.

Among miscellaneous images the most important is that of the Sun-God, Sūrya. After Viṣṇu images those of Sūrya are the most abundant.

An attempt is made in this work to present in a concise form, the information about the Sun-God and his cult that can be gathered from the Sanskrit works, and see how it can be corroborated from the existing monumental remains.

The Sanskrit authorities relied upon for this work mainly Vedic and Puranic writings. Some chapters of the several Purāṇas contain the rules for the making of images. Some of them can be mentioned here:

Agni Purāṇa, Padma Purāṇa, Matsya Purāṇa, Mārkaṇḍeya Purāṇa, Brahma Vaivarta Purāṇa, Viṣṇudharmottara Purāṇa, etc. Some of the Āgamas and the Tantras like Bṛhatsaṁhitā of Varāhamihira, Pūrvakāraṇāgama give descriptions of certain images. Works on art, which were compiled at a later date, also contain matters chiefly relating to these subjects and the names of Śilpaśāstra, Śrī Viśvakarmāvatāraśāstra and Rūpamaṇḍana may be mentioned in this connection. But the descriptions of the images as contained in them may nevertheless be older than this period. It is good to bear in mind that these descriptions were most probably not invented by the authors of the Āgama works under consideration, but were collected from previous authoritative sources. The rules for making of the images must have indeed been formulated at much earlier times and must have long remained unwritten. Texts or portions of texts are, in many cases, the same in two different works, showing that either one borrowed from the other or both drew from a common source. Thus the period covered by this work is from 1500 BC – AD 1200.

In proof of this, it may be mentioned that Varāhamihira, who is known to have lived in the 5th cent. gives descriptions of certain images and that his descriptions are not in any way different from those found in these later Āgama works. The author, Nagnajit, quoted by Varāhamihira, must certainly be older than the middle of the 6th cent. AD the quotation also incidentally informs us that Nagnajit was possibly a south Indian author on Śilpaśāstra and indicates the existence of a school of sculpture in South India. Varāhamihira refers also to another ancient author Vasiṣṭha.

From the actual remains, I have tried to gather information mainly from the Archaeological Survey of India, but I have not neglected the reports or the catalogues of some of the museums like Boston, Mathura, Calcutta, Rajputana, Varendra Research Society (Worcester), Lucknow etc. Attention is paid to the different names of art schools like Graeco-Buddhist, Mathura, Bhājā, Bodhagaya, Gupta, post-Gupta and mediaeval period.

While describing some of the images, I have tried to look at them in the light of certain necessary considerations. First of all, the image is to be described as it is. Its probable origin is also to be traced out. The metaphysical and symbolical meanings, if any, which it bears, are to be made clear. The mythology of the image will have to be explained. The artistic side will also be dealt with as simply as possible. And above all the comparative study of an image, where possible, will have to be offered though not comprehensively.

Hindu deities are often divided into Śaiva, Vaiṣṇava, Śākta, Saura and others. Their relationships are described in the Pauranic, Āgamic and Tantric literature.

The images of gods and goddesses are worshipped by the Hindus not only in the temples, as public places of worship, but also in private households. Since the regular worship of images requires attention to many details in respect of ceremonial purity and piety, such worship is only occasionally conducted in many households, even though the rule is that it should be conducted everyday. Every Hindu household possesses its own images of the family deity (iṣṭa or kula devatā) and ceremonial worship is offered to them in many families only occasionally, though daily bowing down and other practices are followed.

In Vedas this classification is founded on the natural basis which the deities represent and is thus the most practical and least open to objection (comparatively speaking). Rigveda (X.

158-1) which invokes Sūrya, Vāta and Agni for protection from heaven, air and earth respectively is, apparently the lead followed by the predecessors of Yāska whose views are quoted in Nirukta[2] and who held that there are only three representative deities, Sūrya in heaven, Vāyu or Indra in air and Agni on earth, each of these having various appellations according to differences of function.

Sūrya is the most concrete of the heavenly deities, the name (which designates the orb of the sun as well as the god) showing that his character as a luminary was always present in the minds of the poets. As the source of everything that is stationary and moving, he is the soul of the universe. As the all seeing god, he is often called the eye of Mitra, Varuṇa, Agni and other gods. He is also the constant beholder of the good and bad deeds of mortals.

The dawns produce Sūrya and he is said to be the son of the Goddess Aditi. "So often the Ādityas are described as "Aditeḥ Putrāḥ" (sons of Aditi) but this expression might have meant perhaps pre-Vedic parameters as noted by R.C. Majumdar as sons of freedom (like Sāhasāḥ putrāḥ = sons of strength) and probably described as a prominent quality of Varuṇa and other Ādityas.[3] Six Ādityas are enumerated once (Rv. II-27-1), the number being stated as seven and even eight in the last books of the Rv. Among the Ādityas, Varuṇa, Mitra and Aryaman are Indo-Iranian in origin while Bhaga, Dakṣa and Aṁśa seem to be deified abstractions.[4] The sun is probably the seventh Āditya and Mārtaṇḍa the eighth, whom Aditi casts off and brings back; (Rv.-72-8, 9) it is very likely the setting sun. In the Śatapatha Brāhmaṇa, for instance, they are eight in one place and twelve in another and in the latter case it is conceived that they correspond to the twelve months of the year.[5]

---

[2] N. VIII.5.

[3] Majumdar, R.C., *The Vedic Age*, Vol.I, 1951, p. 367.

[4] Ibid., p. 367.

[5] Dhātrā Mitro 'ryamā rudro varuṇaḥ sūrya eva ca/
Bhago Vivasvān puṣā Ca Savitā daśamaḥ Smṛtaḥ//
Ekādaśasthatā Tvaṣṭā Viṣṇurdvādaśa Ucyate/
Compare also Ādityānāmaham Viṣṇuḥ Bg. X-21, Ku Sambhava II-24.

Thus in the time of Brāhmaṇa the number of Ādityas rose to twelve. These twelve suns are supposed to shine only at the destruction of the universe.[6]

In two passages in (Rv.VII-60-1, 62.2) the singer wishes the rising sun to declare him sinless to Mitra, Varuṇa and other gods. This idea probably arose from the fact that the rising sun by his bright light discloses everything that has been done in the darkness of the previous night, and hence it developed into a belief that the sun destroys sins. Kauśitaki[7] is represented to have adored the sun in the morning, at midday and in the evening and having made offerings of water with flowers, sandal, etc. or without (Arghya), prayed for the removal of his sins. And this is what we do or are expected to do in our twilight and midday adorations. Water is sipped by repeating a formula expressive of a wish that the sun, Manyu and Manyupati, may protect the adorer from sins.[8] Āśvalāyana[9] directs that while adoring the morning twilight, one facing the east should repeat the Gāyatrī-Mantra till the whole disc of the sun has risen, and in the evening with his face towards the west till the whole has gone down and the stars have begun to appear.

In the Upanayana ceremony, when the boy is invested with the sacred thread and other badges of a student's life, he is made to look at the orb of the sun, when the preceptor, addressing that deity, prays "Oh God Savitar, this is thy student, protect him. May he not die".[10] Khadir[11] prescribes the adoration of the sun for the enjoyment of riches and for the attainment of fame. The hymn[12] addressed by Yudhiṣṭhira to the sun after he entered his forest-residence and his having obtained a vessel from him for the production of all the food wanted by him, his family and followers, are well-known. In the seventh century the poet Mayūra,

[6] Dagdham Viśvam dahanakiraṇaihrodita dvādaśārkāḥ/ Veṇisaṁhāra III-6.
[7] Kauśitaki Brāhmaṇa Upaniṣad II-7 ..... triṇi upāsanāni bhavanti.
[8] Āśvalāyana Gṛhyasūtra I-3.
[9] Ibid., III-7, 4-6.
[10] Ibid., I.20-6.
[11] *Khadiragrhyasūtra* IV. I,14 and 23.
[12] MBH, Vanaparva, Ad. 262.

who lived at the court of Harṣavardhana, composed Mayūra śataka or Sūrya śataka, a hundred stanzas to obtain relief from leprosy from which he suffered. About the beginning of the eighth century, Bhavabhūti makes the sūtradhāra or the stage-manager of the Mālatimādhava[13] to offer prayers to the rising sun to remove all his sins and bestow blessings on him. Thus the sun has been adored since the Vedic times for the removal of sins and bestowal of riches, food, fame, health and other blessings. At present, twelve prostrations are made to Sūrya by repeating twelve of his names.[14]

It is expected, therefore, that a school would come into existence for the exclusive worship of the sun. And such a school is that of the Sauras. Ānandagiri brings Śankara into contact with the followers of this sect at a place in the south called Subrahmaṇya near Trivendram.[15] The name of their leader was Divākara and they wore a circular spot of red sandal on the forehead and bore red flowers. The substance of the account of this school, given by Divākara, is as follows — "The Supreme Soul, the Sun, is the author of the world. He is the tutelary deity of the Sauras and is adored by them". The Śrutis themselves speak of him as the cause of the world, such as "The Sun is the soul of moveable and immovable things" (Rv. I-115-1) and "That Āditya is Brahman". Brahman, with which the sun has thus been identified, is the cause of the whole world, according to the text[16] from which all these beings originate etc." There is also a Smṛti text in favour of this doctrine. There are six classes of devotees of the sun all bearing a mark made by red sandal, wearing a garland of red flowers and repeating the formula of eight syllables.[17] "Some worship the orb of the sun who has just risen as Brahmadeva, the creator, others the sun on the meridian as Iśvara and the setting sun the destroyer. He is also regarded as the originator. Some, regard the setting sun as Viṣṇu the protector and

[13] Act I verse 3.
[14] Bhandarkar, R.G., *Vaiṣṇavism and Śaivism* (Sect. 114).
[15] Ibid.
[16] Taittirīya Upaniṣad (III-i-i).
[17] Bhargo devasya dhimahi.

cause of the creation, destruction and highest entity as well , worship him.

There are some who resort to all the three positions on the sun, as a triple form. Others, observing the vow of regularly seeing the orb, adore the Supreme Soul as existing in it with golden whiskers and golden hair. One section of this class is devoted simply to the vow of the observation of the disc and they see the orb, worship it in the sixteen ways, dedicate all their actions to the god and do not eat without seeing the orb. The devotees of the sixth class imprint the orb on their forehead, arms and bosom with a heated iron piece and meditate on the God in their minds continuously. All these six classes have to repeat the same Mantra, or formula of eight syllables. The followers of this creed like other sectarians interpret various Vedic texts as setting forth the greatness and the supremacy of their own God."[18] The Puruṣa Sūkta (Rv. X-90) and the Śatarudriya are so expounded and the conclusion is that all, who desire emancipation should adore the sun, should bear his marks on the body and mutter the Mantra.

The unpopularity of sun-images may have been due to the fact that the solar-deity itself was visible daily to everybody and there was no need for its representation. The masses worshipped the solar-deity not in its anthropomorphic but symbolic forms of disc, wheel, lotus etc.

In Gujarat, sun is worshipped as Sūrya-Nārāyaṇa. The Sun-God was the most popular deity in this country (in pre-Mohamedan times). This cult has, however, merged into Vaiṣṇavism. But now-a-days the worship of the Sun-God as an important national festival has disappeared but the Hindu ladies of the country still observe a *Vrata* (or woman's festival) in honour of Sūrya and the *Vrata* of Māgha-maṇḍala. Still the most popular Vrata, which the Bengali girls observe for years together before their marriage, is essentially a phase of solar worship. By many, the Holi festival in the south of India is believed to have been instituted originally in order to propitiate the Sun-God. He is invoked to heal diseases

[18] Bhandarkar, R.G., *Vaiṣṇavism and Śaivism* (Sec. 115).

and on the occasion of an eclipse and other ceremonies observed to rescue the deity from the powers of evil. The same concept that worship and sacrifice are efficacious to avert disaster from the object of worship may perhaps be recognised in the special frequency of sun-ritual and adoration in the winter season among some northern tribes, at a time when the divinity may be supposed to be weak. A sacred meal is partaken of in his honour and this must be eaten without salt. On the day of transit of the sun at the Tropic of Capricorn (i.e. the 14th January), men worship the Sun and women offer to Brāhmaṇas and other married women of their caste, materials required for the dressing, such as, red powder boxes, bangles, mirrors, combs, etc. There are peoples in India, at the present time,who believe themselves to have descended from the sun.

This indicates, indigenous growth. But such an influence undoubtedly, contributed to the growth of the sun-worship prevalent in Northern India from the early centuries of the Christian era. Varāhamihira (Bṛhatsaṁhitā, Chap. 60, Verse 19) tells us that the installation and consecration of the images and the temples of the sun must have been established by the Magas, who are none other than the sun and fire-worshipping Magi of ancient Iran, and generally, those who worship a certain deity according to their special ritual should be made to perform the ceremony concerning that deity. This shows that the Magas were, according to Varāhamihira, the special priests of the Sun-God. The Purāṇas like Bhaviṣya, Sāmba, Varāha and others, narrate the story of the introduction of the cult into India from Śakadvipa (Eastern Iran). There is a legend concerning this matter in the Bhaviṣya Purāṇa (Chap. 139) — Sāmba, the son of Kṛṣṇa by Jambuvati, constructed a temple of the sun on the banks of the Candrabhāgā, the modern Chenab, in Punjab and no local brāhmaṇa would accept the office of a regular priest of the temple. He thereupon asked Gauramukha, the priest of Ugrasena to get Magas, who were the special sun-worshippers, from Śakadvīpa. Then is given the history of the Magas. Sujihva was a Brāhmaṇa of the Mihira Gotra. He had a daughter of the name

Nikṣubhā, with whom the sun fell in love. The son, of these two, was called Jaraśabda or Jaraśasta and from him sprang all Magas. They wore a girdle round their waist which was called Avyanga. Thereupon Sāmba went on the back of Garuḍa, his father's vehicle to Śakadvīpa, brought some Magas from there and installed them to the offices of priests of the temple he had constructed. The Magas have long since known in the literary history of India. "There is one inscription at Govindapur, in the Gaya district, dated Śaka 1059 corresponding to 1137–38 AD in the opening stanza of which the Magas, who sprang from the sun, are represented to have been brought into the country by Sāmba. Six great poets, the works of some of whom are extant, are also mentioned. There are traces of the Magas elsewhere and there are brāhmaṇas of that name in Rajputana, Gujarat and some other provinces of Northern India. These Magas are the Maghavan of ancient Persia. The name Jaraśasta mentioned above as occurring in the Bhaviṣyapurāṇa connects them with the Avesta prophet Zarathushtra. The Avyanga which according to the Purāṇa they wore round their waist, was the same as the Aivyaonghen of the Avesta language, which last signifies the *Kusti* worn by the Parasees to the present day. Alberuni, speaking of the Persian priests Magians, says that they existed in India and were called Magas.[19] The idea of locating them on a continent called Śakadvīpa must have arisen from the fact that they were like the Śakas with whom the Indians were familiar since the second or third century before the Christian era as inhabitants to the west of the India. Evidently the worship of the sun or Mihira-worship was brought into India by Magi, but at whose instance and under what circumstances they came, it is difficult to say. The legends of their having been brought by Sāmba was current in the first half of the 12th century, as we have seen from the inscription.

An inscription at Mandasor records the construction of a temple to the sun in the year AD 437–38 by a guild of weavers

[19] Sachau's translation, Vol.1, p. 21.

and its repair in the year AD 473–74. Another on a copper plate found at Indore, in Bulandshahar District in the United Provinces, mentions an endowment of Devaviṣṇu in AD 464 for lighting a lamp in a temple of the sun. And in a third is recorded a grant in AD 511 to a temple of Āditya or the sun. A great many more temples have been discovered especially in Western India from Multan to Kutch and Northern Gujarat.[20] The ruins of one exists at Moḍherā, eighteen miles to the south of Pāṭaṇa (Gujarat) and they contain the date Vikram Saṁvat 1083 corresponding to AD1027 and its earlier existence has some evidence. There was another at Gwalior, constructed in the time of Mihirakula, the Huṇa prince, in the beginning of the 6th cent. AD.[21] The Huṇas-Toramāṇa and Mihirakula were both worshippers of the sun.

Sāmba[22], a son of Śri Kṛṣṇa was suffering from leprosy, to cure his disease, he worshipped Sūrya (sun). Some Brāhmins of Śakadvīpa were the worshippers of Sūrya. We find this story in detail in Bhaviṣya Purāṇa. The Western Kṣtrapas who ruled over Gujarat in the first century of the Christian era, were worshipping the sun. They are Indo-Scytheans. The reference to a private sun-temple in a copper plate of king Śilāditya I[23] further supports the existence of sun-worship. The Gurjar kings — King Dadda I and Dadda II — who were in possession of land in the vicinity of Bharukaccha were also devotees of the sun during that period. The word 'Maitraka' itself is believed by some to have been derived from 'mitra', the sun, and is taken to be supported by the ending word 'Āditya' as in Śilāditya. However, out of about twenty Valabhi kings only the fifth king Dharapaṭṭa seems to have professed the faith of the sun, as he styled himself as 'Paramādītya-bhakta'. These references we find in many inscriptions. Among the kings of Kanauj, three kings (7th to 10th cent.) were also Āditya-bhakta.[24] In this cult, the Iranian influence was

[20] *Architectural Antiquities of Northern Gujarat.*
[21] Bhandarkar, R.G., *Vaiṣṇavism and Śaivism* (Sec. 116).
[22] Bhaviṣya Purāṇa (Chap. 139).
[23] Bühler, Dhānk Plates of 200, A. IX, p. 237.
[24] Hall, in the preface of the Vāsavadattā.

not considered foreign, during the middle ages due to close contact. In short, this cult was very well known in the whole of India.

The sun is the basis in astronomy and astrology. Some writers start their work after praying to the Sun-God. Now, we do not find any Āditya-bhakta or Saura even in the south of India. They are a very small in number. Yet the prayer to the Sun-God is in vogue and many Hindus still worship the sun.

Three

DESCRIPTION OF THE SUN IMAGES IN SANSKRIT LITERATURE

We have seen in the previous chapters that in the earliest Indian literature, the Rigveda, the gods, being personifications of natural phenomena, were often anthropomorphic. To the imagination of the poets of the hymns the gods were outwardly differentiated mainly by the weapons they wielded or the animals which drew their cars. Thus Sūrya in Rv. is described as the soul or the guardian of all that moves or is stationary (1-115[1], 7-60[2]). He has a car which is drawn by one steed or by an infinite number of steeds (I-115[3], 10-37[3].49[7]) or by seven horses (V-45[9]) or mares called haritaḥ (I.50[8-9], 7.60[3]).

Sūrya's path is prepared for him by Varuṇa (I-24[8], 7.87) or by the Ādityas, Mitra, Varuṇa, Aryamān (7.60[4]). Pūṣan is his messenger (6.58[3]). The Dawn or Dawns reveal Sūrya as well as Agni and the Sacrifice (7.80[2]). He shines forth from the lap of the dawn i.e. he, as the son of the sky and the dawn (7.63[8]). But from another point of view Dawn is Sūrya's wife[1] (7.75[5]). Sūrya's horses represent his rays (which are seven in number, 8.61[16]). His seven mares are called the daughters of his car (I.50[9]). From this description, it can be said that as early as the Rigveda anthropomorphic traits came to be attached to the Sun-God. In the Rv. the sun is not a maleficent power and for this aspect of the luminary only passages from the Atharvaveda (name of Divākar) and the literature of the Brāhmaṇas can be quoted.[2]

Now in later literature, Sūrya is regarded both as one of the twelve Ādityas, presiding over the months, or as one of the Nava-grahas or 'nine planets'.

All the Ādityas and Navagrahas may be iconographically

---

[1] Taittirīya Saṁhitā, IV, 3-11.

[2] Macdonell, *Vedic Mythology*, p. 3.

represented and made the object of a cult. The cult of the sun, which is by far the most important, is closely connected with that of Viṣṇu, who is identified with the sun in the Vedas. The special worship of Sūrya was well known to the Vedic Āryan, and Iranian can be seen from these sources.

Now the nine planets Sūrya, Candra, Bhauma, Budha, Śūkra, Bṛhaspati, Śani, Rāhu and Ketu are also worshipped by the Hindus and their images are generally found in all important Śaiva temples in South India.[3] They are invariably placed in a separate maṇḍapa having a pediment of about three feet in height and no two of them are made to face each other.

It is assumed that the images of the planets are set up in temples in the order in which they are in the Zodiacal circle at the time of the construction of the temple. If there is any truth in this assumption, these planet figures may serve as a new means for calculating the probable dates of the construction of the temples wherein they are installed for worship. Further work is essential to verify this assumption.

Regarding the worship of Sūrya in ancient times in India Nagendranatha Vasu has collected much valuable information in his Archaeological Survey of Mayūra-bhañja. He attempts to prove that the Magas or Scythic Brāhmaṇas were the first to introduce the worship of the Sun in India. However, it may be pointed out that the worship of the Sun was well-known in India from the Vedic period and in it some element from Iranian sources were incorporated. As we have seen above (in Bhaviṣya Purāṇa) that Sāmba, one of the sons of Śrī Kṛṣṇa was suffering from leprosy and that he was cured of it by worshipping Sūrya and that some Brāhmaṇas of the Śakadvīpa were worshippers of that deity. The same (Bhaviṣya) Purāṇa relates "that Zarathustra, who acknowledged the superiority of fire, was born of that element. He also used to interpret the Veda in a perverted way, which led to a quarrel between him and the Magas who worshipped Mitra, the Sun-God". N. Vasu adds further "In the Zend

[3] Rao, Gopinatha, *Elements of Hindu Iconography*, Vol.I, p. 299.

Avesta the oldest record of the fire-worshippers, Mitra is known as only one of the minor gods. But on the other hand in Mihir Yast, we find a faint reference to the effect that at one time Mitra was worshipped as the highest God. Some of the Mitra worshippers, the Śākadvīpa Brāhmaṇas migrated to India with their families."

The description of Mitra or the Sun-God, as taken from the Viśvakarmā Śilpa, is given by N. Vasu in the following words — "His great chariot has one wheel[4] and is drawn by seven horses, he has a lotus in each hand, wears an armour and has a shield over his breast, has beautiful straight hair, is surrounded by a halo of light, has good hair and apparel, is decorated with gold ornaments and jewels, has on his right side the figure of Nikshubhā and on the left that of Rājñī[5] (Queen) with all sorts of ornaments and whose hair and necklace are bright." His chariot mentioned above is called by the name of Makaradhvaja. He wears a crown. The figure is surrounded by a halo. Daṇḍa[6] (Yama) is represented as one-faced and Skanda as having a bright conch-shell, these two figures with the form of man are placed in front. Vārcha[7] on a lotus is placed or on a horse. His body is represented as lustrous and he is the one who gives light to all the worlds. A Sūrya-maṇḍala is to be made by placing nutmeg and vermilion. He (Mitra) has four hands or only two. In both of his hands there are lotuses. He is seated on a chariot

---

[4] Pandey, Lalita Prasad, *Sun Worship in Ancient India*, p. 69, Delhi, 1971. Compare – The chariot has only one wheel (There is a Vedic myth which tells us that one wheel of the chariot of the Sun-God was taken by Indra, therefore his chariot is always shown with only one wheel).

[5] Here Rājñī is taken as queen. It, however, appears to be the name of the goddess associated with Sūrya or his wife. Compare – Viṣṇudharmottara Khaṇḍa III, Ad. 67, verse 10.

[6] Here Daṇḍa means Yama. From the description found in the Bhaviṣyapurāṇa as well as Vishṇudharmottara, it appears to be probable that Daṇḍa is evidently a contraction of Daṇḍanāyaka, the commander-in-chief of the celestial hosts and should therefore be understood to refer to skanda.

[7] Here the reading Vārcha does not give any sense and also the translation given above is not correct. Instead of *Vārcha* it should be Vārka and it means either Arka (Sūrya) should be seated on the horse or on the Padma (lotus).

drawn by horses of variegated colour. His two door keepers Daṇḍa (Yama) & Piñgala (Agni) have swords in their hands."[8]

In the Bhaviṣya-Purāṇa[9] it is stated that Sūrya began to burn the asuras with his heat, the latter thereupon attacked Sūrya. The gods then felt bound to help Sūrya and with this object in view they placed the attendants Skanda on the left of Sūrya and Agni on the right. Since Skanda is the punisher of the wicked in the universe, he is called Daṇḍa-nāyaka, and from his reddish yellow colour Agni, the god of fire, obtains the name Piñgala. The same authority also gives the names of the attendants of Sūrya as Rājña and Śrauṣa, and identifies these with Skanda and Śiva respectively. The names are also derived and explained therein. "Because Skanda (Kārtikeya) shines always as the commander of the army of the celestials, he is known by the name of Rājña". Such is the explanation of the name Rājña, which is here evidently conceived to be derived from the root 'Rāj', meaning to shine. The explanation of the name Śrauṣa, the root 'Sru', is known to be employed to denote movement and to this the suffix 'Sa' is added. Because he goes, he is known by the alternative appellation of Śrauṣa. It is worthy to note here that Vasu has pointed out that the name of the attendant of the sun, as known in the Avesta, is Sraoshavareza or simply srosh sometimes. The same Bhaviṣyapurāṇa adds further that the Aśvinidevatās may also be made to be standing, one on each side of Sūrya or on the

[8] Viśvakarmā śilpa Ms. pp. 306-31a quoted by Mayurbhanja, Archaeological Survey p. XVI. Ekachakram sasaptaśvam sasārathim Mahāratham/Hasta dvayam padmadharam Kancukścarmavakṣasam// Akuncita sukeshastu Prabhā maṇḍala maṇḍitam/ Keshaveshasamāyuktam svarṇaratna Vibhūṣitam/Nikṣubhā dakṣine Pārśve vāme rājñi Prakīrtitā// Sarvābharaṇasaṁyuktā Keshahārasamujjvalā// Evamuktarathastasya makaradhvaja is yate/ Makuṭañcāpi dātavyamanyat sarvam maṇḍalam/ Ekavaktrāṅkito daṇḍasskandastejokarāmbujam(?) Kṛtvā tu sthāpayet pūrvam puruṣākṛtirūpiṇau// Hayārūḍhastu (?ntu) Kurvīt padmasthami Vārcha(?) nāmakam// Sadīvya mānavapuṣam Sarvalokaika dīpakam// Jāti hi ṅgulya Saṁsthāpya (?) Kārayet Sūryamaṇḍalam/ Caturbāhurdvihasto Vā rekhā maṇi Vibhājanā// Dvihastastha Sarojanma Śabalāśvaratha sthitaḥ/ Daṇḍaśca Piñgalaśchaiva dvārapālau ca khadginau// See also Elements of Hindu Iconography Vol.I, pt.II, p. 302.

[9] Bhaviṣya Purāṇa, Ad. 139.

right of Sūrya, there might be Piñgala with an inkpot and a pen and on the left Daṇḍi with a daṇḍa in his hand. The Goddesses Rājñī and Nikṣubhā are also required to be made to stand on either side of Sūrya. It is said that these two goddesses represent the air and the earth.

In the temple of Sūrya or the Sun-God, Soma and the other grahas should be, it is said, established in the following manner: In the east there should be Soma, in the south-east Bhauma, in the south Bṛhaspati, in the south-west Rāhu, in the west Śukra, in the north-west Ketu, in the north Budha and in the north-east Śani. The names of the door-keepers, at the four gates of the temple of Sūrya, are given thus in the Bhaviṣya-purāṇa; those at the first gate are called *Dharma* and *Artha*; at the second *Garuḍa* and *Yama*; at the third *Kubera* and *Vināyaka* and at the fourth *Raivata* and *Diṇḍi*.

According to the South Indian texts, the Aṁsumadbhedāgama[10] and the Suprabhedāgama, the figure of the Sun-God should be sculptured with two hands, each holding a lotus. The hands should be held up so as to cause the fists holding the lotuses reach the level of the shoulders. His head is to be surrounded by a halo (Kāntimaṇḍala) and he should be adorned with many ornaments; on his head there should be a Karaṇḍamakuṭa, and the garment worn by him should be red in colour. He should wear a pair of ruby ear-rings (Kuṇḍalas) and over his chest there should be a necklace (Hāra). He should wear only one cloth and the body should be covered (with a coat) as 'northern' style. The fabric of this coat should be so delicate in texture as to make portions of the body visible through it. There should also be a Yajñopavīta on his person. The figure of Sūrya should be made to stand on a padma-pīṭha by itself or should be placed in a hexagonal chariot drawn by seven horses fully caparisoned. The chariot should have only one wheel and be shown to be driven by the lame Aruṇa. At the right side of Sūrya there should stand Uṣā and on the left Pratyuṣā. A second authority mentions

[10] Rao, Gopinatha, *Elements of Hindu Iconography,* Vol.I, Part II, p. 306ff.

four consorts of Sūrya; namely Rājñī, Suvarṇā, Suvarcasā and Chāyā or one half of the body of Sūrya taken vertically, should have the shape of a dark complexioned woman, probably indicating that the sun in spite of his being the God of Light, is inseparably wedded to night and its darkness.

The Śilparatna (Adhyāya 25) describes the sun as red-coloured, full of lustre, having three eyes and well ornamented. He holds black and red lotus in his hands. His chariot is drawn by seven horses with the ropes in the form of serpents. The chariot has only one wheel. Sūrya has two dwārapālas on each side of him. They are named as Maṇḍala[11] and Piñgala. According to this same authority the materials, of which the crown (Kiriṭa) and the ear-rings (Kuṇḍalas) are made, should be Padmarāga (topaz) and Māṇikya (ruby). The Maṇḍala (Daṇḍa ?) and Piñgala should hold in their hands a rod and a sword.

Bṛhatsaṁhitā (Adhyāya 58) gives the instruction that, in sculpturing the image of Āditya, attention has to be paid to the nose, the forehead, the chest, the knees, the thighs and the neck. They should all be raised and prominent. The diameter of the halo should be twice the height of the Kiriṭa. If the figure made is to be of one cubit height it should be a Saumyamūrti, that is, a handsome, gentle figure. If it be of two cubits, it would be productive of wealth; if it be of three or four cubits, it would bestow happiness and prosperity. The general description of the Sun-God corresponds with the descriptions given in other similar texts.

The Viṣṇudharmottara (Khaṇḍa III, Ad. 67) gives full details of the Sun-icons. According to this authority, the sun has four arms and he should wear a northerner's dress and wear an armour. He wears a girdle, known as Yāviyāṅga[12] He is as red as sindūra (vermilion) and has a good form. He has a fine moustache and is dressed with all the ornaments. In his left and right hands there should be reins. He is decorated with garlands made

[11] The correct reading should be Daṇḍa and not Maṇḍala.

[12] Yāviyāṅga is the same as avyanga, the girdle worn by Maga priests.

of all kinds of flowers.

Daṇḍa,[13] having an anthropomorphic form, should be placed on his left and Piñgala of a deep tawny colour on his right.

Both should wear dresses of northern style. The remaining two hands of the Sun-God should be on the heads of these two. Piñgala carries a leaf and a pen in his hands. Daṇḍa has a shield (lit. leather) and a trident (Śūla) in his hands. On the left side of the Sun-God should be placed a banner having an emblem of lion.[14]

His four sons Revanta, Yama and two Manus should be placed on his two sides. His four wives Rājñī, Rikṣubhā, Chāyā and Suvarcalā should also be placed on his two sides. The Sun, who is the lord of planets, should be surrounded by the planets.

His chariot has one wheel, six spokes and is drawn by seven horses. His charioteer is Aruṇa. He should be represented as seated in a chariot.

Coming to the significance of his emblems, this authority says, that his seven horses are seven metres. They are Gāyatrī, Uṣṇik, Anuṣṭubh, Bṛhati, Pankti, Triṣṭubh and Jagati. With the reins in his hands, he supports the entire universe, the lion on his banner represents Dharma in person. The Sun holds the entire world by his girdle. His four wives Rājñī, Rikṣubhā,[15] Chāyā and Suvarcalā[16] represent the earth (Bhū), the sky (Dyau), the shadow (Chāyā) and the lustre (Prabhā) respectively. He is red because he is the source of all lustre and his limbs are concealed under unbearable lustre. The Sun is all light. Thus the text explains the inner symbolism of the features of the Sun-images.

In the description of the image of the Sun-God, two important points of historical significance are to be noted; the dress of Sūrya and those of Daṇḍa and Piñgala are of udīcya type. His

---

[13] Here Daṇḍa is the abbreviated form of Daṇḍanāyaka, the commander-in-chief.

[14] In Viśvakarmaśilpa the emblem of the Sun is Makara and not *lion*. Makar-adhvaja is always for the God of love (Kāmadeva).

[15] The correct reading should be Nikṣubhā.

[16] The name Suvarcalā has no sense. It should be Suvarcasā. Varcasā means lustre and hence the meaning.

girdle is called Aviyānga or Viyānga or Yāviyānga which will be discussed afterwards.

It is true that iconography and temples are two connected spheres where they appear to have exerted powerful influence. Though there might have been native tradition of image-making and temple-building for different sectarian[17] gods; yet it appears that the images and temples of the Sun-God were either not known, or if known, were not popular in India before the advent of the Magas, as is evidenced by the Purāṇas.[18] But, it will be interesting to see the iconography of the temples of Viṣṇudharmottara (Khaṇḍa III, Ad. 86) with the iconography of the Sun in the same work.

A specific shape of the temple, is closely connected with the shape and name of its deity, as are the Linga and Garuḍa temples. It resembles the bird Garuḍa having two wings. These have the shape of attached shrines; the main building of the temple forms the body of Garuḍa, the Sun-bird, who carries Sūrya, the Sun. The temple here, has the shape of the Vāhana (vehicle) and thus, is similar in its function of conveying divinity to those temples, which were built in the likeness of the chariots of the Gods (Ad. 86, verses 61-62).

The Sun temple, Garuḍa houses the image of Sūrya, in the central building. It is flanked in the lateral shrines by Daṇḍa and Piñgala or by Saturn and Śukra or by Keśava and Śiva. This is its primary destination. In it, however, other gods too were enshrined and their 'lateral' divinities. They are: Candra — the Moon, Kāma, Indra, Yama, Varuṇa and Kubera. They are connected with and, thus, are substituted for Sūrya. Garuḍa, himself, the bird-form and Vāhana of the Sun, has also his image enshrined as the main divinity; he is flanked by Kaśyapa and Vinatā (Verses.63-73).

---

[17] Pāṇini and Patañjali informs us about the images of Hindu sectarian gods.

[18] Sāmba Purāṇa 29, 2-6. It is interesting to note that here the Maga priests are not described as responsible for image-making but Viśvakarman, the native architect was responsible. It is suggested that Bodhagaya, Bhājā etc. represented the native tradition of solar iconography. See Banerjee, J.N., *Development of Hindu Iconography,* pp. 432-34.

Sūrya and his attendants are substituted, not only by gods of the family of the sun, but also by one of the three great gods, Brahmā, Śiva or Vāsudeva and their lateral divinities. Vāsudeva may be accompanied by Rudra (Śiva) and Brahmā, or also by Garuḍa and Ananta, or also by Garuḍa and Aruṇa, the Vāhana and the charioteer of Sūrya. (Verses.74-76).

To whichever god the temple Garuḍa is dedicated, it is a temple of Sūrya, which shines in all these images. Dharma in the main temple, and Artha and Kāma in its wings, may also be worshipped in this temple. (Ad. 86 Verses 77) The purpose of its construction like that of any temple is to attain Mokṣa.[19]

This description of the temple, however, has still to be investigated by archaeologists.

The Matsya Purāṇa (Ad. 261) describes the image of Sūrya thus — "Sūrya", the image should carry the lotuses in the two hands. He should be adorned with the ornaments. His mukuṭa should be made up of variegated rubies. His chariot has one wheel and seven horses. His horses are lustrous and tied with the serpents, in the forms of ropes. He has two dvārapālas by the name of Daṇḍa and Piṅgala. They should hold a sword and pen in their hands respectively. Thus, the Sun-God should be surrounded with all different gods. His charioteer is Aruṇa.

The description of his chariot is given thus: the sun moves on his one-wheeled chariot swiftly, drawn by his horses, and at the end of a day returns to his abode. He always has (tawny) greenish yellow horses, yoked to his chariot. He drinks water through thousands of his rays and ceases to draw it, when it passes the point of saturation, he discharges them in the form of rain.

The sun, in one entire day goes swiftly over the world, consisting of the seven oceans and seven islands, seated in his one-wheeled chariot and drawn by seven horses. The seven horses yoked to the Sun's chariot are no other than the seven chandas (metres); they can assume forms according to their will; they go

---

[19] Viśvakarmaprakāśa (VI-10).

as they like; their speed is swift as wind, their colour is tawny and being one yoked they go on incessantly; they never get tired. They are the gods declaring the glory of Brahmā. Ascending on such a chariot, the sun traverses the earth in course of one day (twenty-four hours).

Thus, the sun is carried on by the horses flying like birds. He is honoured by Gandharvas, Apsaras and demons with Gīta (music) and Nṛtya (dance).

Similar description of the Sūrya-Ratha (The chariot of the sun) is given in the Brahmāṇḍa Purāṇa (Ad. 23).[20]

According to Agni Purāṇa (Ad. 51), the sun is described as having lotuses in his hands and having a chariot with seven horses. On his right side there should be Daṇḍi[21] holding in his hands the writing materials — the inkpot and a pen; and on his left there should be Piñgala holding a staff in his hand. On the side of Sūrya there should be Rājñī and Niṣprabhā[22] holding in their hands chowries (Bālavyajana).[23] Thus, the Sun is surrounded with a group. Or the Sun should be alone, mounted on the horse-back with the lotus and granting a boon (Varada) Mudrā. All the door-keepers should be with the Mudgara (club), Śūla (spear), Cakra (disc) and a flower Abja (lotus). Another type of the sun image is to be found in the Śāradātilaka.[24] It is very interesting and worth to be noted. According to this, the image of the Sun should be represented as having four heads and

[20] The description given in Rao, Gopinatha, *Elements of Hindu Iconography* is quite unreliable. He gives the description of the sun under the name of the Matsya Purāṇa. But one cannot find the same description given in Matsya Purāṇa itself. His description quite agrees with the description given in Viṣṇudharmottara. But Rao does not mention the name of Viṣṇu-dharmottara in the text and in the appendix he gives some references from the Sanskrit texts regarding Ādityāḥ. Here also, he has mixed the two texts — Viṣṇudharmottara and Matsya Purāṇa.

[21] Here the implements in the hands of Daṇḍa and Piñgala seem quite contrary.

[22] Niṣprabhā means lustreless or pale-looking. It is very difficult to understand whether it is the name miswritten for Nikṣubhā or the adjective of Rājñī.

[23] For the first time we see here the queens with chowries.

[24] Caturvaktra Sūryadhyānam/ Sāradātilaka... quoted in Śrītattwanidhi, p. 121.

eight hands. No such statue is known to have been discovered as yet.

According to the Viṣṇu Purāṇa[25] (Ad. 8), the seven horses of the Sun's car are the metres of the Vedas, namely, Gāyatrī, Bṛhati, Uṣṇis, Jagatī, Triṣṭubh, Anuṣṭubh and Pankti. The same authority (in Ad. 10) says that His (Sun's) car is presided over by divine Ādityas, Rishis, heavenly singers and nymphs, Yakṣas, serpents and Rākṣasas (one of each being placed in it every month). The Āditya — Dhātri, the sage — Pulastya, the Gandharva —Tumburu, the nymph — Kratusthalā, the Yakṣa—Rathakṛta, the serpent — Vāsuki and the Rākṣasa — Heti, always reside in the Sun's car in the month of Madhu or Caitra as its seven guardians. In this manner, Maitreya, a troop of seven celestial beings, supported by the energy of Viṣṇu, occupies during the several months the orb of the sun. The sage celebrates his praise and the Gandharva sings and the nymph dances before him; the Rākṣasa attends upon his steps, the serpent harnesses his steeds and the Yakṣa trims the reins; the numerous pigmy sages, the Bālakhilyas, ever surrounded his chariot. The whole troop of seven, attached to the Sun's car, are the agents in the distribution of cold, heat and rain at their respective seasons.

Now Bhaviṣya Purāṇa gives one interesting story for the origin of avyanga in connection with the troop of the seven. It is as follows: During each ṛtu (season) there came to the Sūrya-maṇḍala, one each from among the Ṛṣis, Devatās, Nāgas, Gandharvas, Apsaras, Yakṣas and Rākṣasas. In one of these turns Vāsuki, the Nāga presented Sūrya with a cord, called the avyanga, or ahyanga which was produced from his body. This cord was composed of gold and had the colour half-white and half-red. From this time onwards the followers of the Sūrya-cult were required to wear a similar cord round their loins.

Similar description of the image of the sun, can be found in the following texts: Padmapurāṇa (Ad. 75, 76), Sūryopaniṣad, Sāmba Purāṇa (Ad. 6), Chaturvargacintamaṇi (Ad. 5 in the

[25] Wilson, H., *The Viṣṇupurāṇa.*

Dānakhaṇḍa...), Mārkaṇḍeya Purāṇa, Varāha Purāṇa (Ad. 26), Kūrma Purāṇa (Ad. 18), Samarāngaṇa Sūtradhāra (Ad. 5).

As we have already seen, the Ādityas are twelve in number and each of them is said to preside over a month of the year. Their names are given variously in various works, and a good many of them agree in naming them in order, as Dhātri, Mitra, Aryaman, Rudra, Varuṇa, Sūrya, Bhaga, Vivasvān, Puṣan, Savitṛ, Tvaṣṭṛ and Viṣṇu. The image of each of these twelve Ādityas, is described in the Viśvakarmaśāstra[26] and the description in so far as it relates to their hands and the objects to be carried in them, may conveniently be summarised in the form of a table as follows:

Names of the Ādityas	Back Right Hand	Back Left Hand	Front Right Hand	Front Left Hand
1. Dhātrī	Kamalamālā	Kamaṇḍalu	Lotus	Lotus
2. Mitra	Candra	Śūla	Lotus	Lotus
3. Aryaman	Cakra	Gadā (Kaumodakī)	Lotus	Lotus
4. Rudra	Akṣamālā	Cakra	Lotus	Lotus
5. Varuṇa	Cakra	Pāṣa	Lotus	Lotus
6. Sūrya	Kamaṇḍalu	Akṣamālā	Lotus	Lotus
7. Bhaga	Śūla	Cakra	Lotus	Lotus
8. Vivasvān	Śūla	Puṣpamālā	Lotus	Lotus
9. Pūṣan	Padma (lotus)	Padma (lotus)	Lotus	Lotus
10. Savitṛ	Gadā	Cakra	Lotus	Lotus
11. Tvaṣṭṛ	Mālā	Homajakalikā	Lotus	Lotus
12. Viṣṇu	Cakra	Padma	Lotus	Lotus

Of these Mitra, it is said, should have three eyes; Rudra is considered to be important Āditya. Puṣan is required to be sculptured beautifully; he is declared to be destroyer of all sins. Savitṛ is the Āditya who is capable of fulfilling the wishes of his devotees and bestowing boons on them. Of all the Ādityas the most lustrous one is Viṣṇu.[27] Though Viṣṇu is the youngest of the

[26] See Khare, G.H., *Mūrtivijñana* (Marathi), 1939, p. 139.

[27] Ādityānāmaham Viṣṇuḥ, see Bhagavadgītā Ad.10-21 and Kumārasaṁbhava II-24.

Āditya, yet he is the greatest due to his qualities.[28] In the Atharvaveda Āditya the Sun-God has been identified with Viṣṇu[29]. It is interesting to note here, that the names of some of the Ādityas according to the Indian Āryas are the same, as those according to Iranian Āryas; the Mitra, Aryaman and Bhaga of the Hindus are identical with the Mitra, Aryaman and Bhaga or Bagho of the Parsees.

We can conclude, from the above given description of the Sun-God, that the two types of the sun images described in the Sanskrit texts are: (i) he is seated on a lotus, has two hands holding lotuses, moving in a car drawn by seven horses; and (ii) he has either four or two hands holding lotuses, moving in a car drawn by seven horses. The charioteer, the legless Aruṇa, is driving the horses. He is attended by two or four male figures, and two or four female figures. Their names differ according to different Sanskrit books. Generally, the female figures are his queens. In male figures, sometimes, they are his sons or his bodyguards or the Dvārapālas.

Now it is necessary to note here some Sanskrit words, which are used so often in connection with Sūrya: Kiriṭa, Kavaca and Kañcuka.

The words Kiriṭa and Mukuṭa are used in the sense of head-dress. So, Sūrya is called Kiriṭin. Hence we can derive its meaning as "One who wears Kiriṭa is called *Kiriṭin,* as the word *Pītāmbara* for Viṣṇu". The etymology of the word is accepted in the Sanskrit literature. Hemacandra tries to explain this word from the root Krū — Kiryate, and *Amarakośa* derives it from kṛ Kirati which is quite obscure, while *Pāṇini* tries to explain it as Kṛtṝkṛṣibhyakiṭan (Unādi-6). It is used so often for Viṣṇu, Indra, Arjuna and for Sūrya. So, the word Kiriṭa can be taken as in the general sense, that who puts on Kiriṭa is called Kiriṭin.[30]

The word *Kavaca* and *Kañcuka* means the coat of mail. We,

---

[28] MBH, I.65, 15-16.

[29] Av. XVII, 1-8.

[30] Kiriṭinām gadinām Cakriṇām Ca tejorāṣim Sarvato diptimantam (Bhagwad Gītā Ad. XI, verse 17 and Ad. XI, verse 35).

so often, find the words *Kavaca* and *Kañcuka* in connection with Sūrya to explain *Udīcyaveśa* i.e. the dress of a northerner. We try to find the origin or the etymology of these words.

Kavaca: Pāṇini derives this word Kavaca from the roots *Ku*, Kū (3rd and Ist conjugation, Unādi 4-2) with the suffix *asa* or *aca* make *Kavasa* or *Kavaca.* But the etymology of these words are doubtful. Kavaca may signify "the coat of mail, armour". In the Atharvaveda (XI-10-72), the word *Kavacin* is taken in the sense of one who wears Kavaca, while in Rigveda (VII-18-12) the word Kavasa is the name of one of the Rishis. The Atharvaveda gives also the word *Kavaca-pāśa,* in the sense of the jacket of the sun. These words may be of the non-Aryan origin.

Kañcuka: The word Kañcuka, according to Pāṇini is derived from the root Kañc ātmanepada of the first conjugation. Here, the root Kañc with a termination *U* and the suffix *Ka* form the word Kañcuka. The words Kaca means hair, Kuca means breast, Kakṣa means tying up the lower garment — dhotī, Kukshī — the stomach, Kavaca — an armour, Kañcuka — a jacket, a dress fitting close to the upper part of the body, armour, mail, a cuirass; the skin of the snake (non-Aryan origin).

Moreover, there are many South Indian texts, such as, Aṁśumadbhedāgama and Suprabhedāgama, which do not mention these alien features.[31] The South Indian images of the Sun-God are on these lines, as they are free from Iranian features. Reference may be made, to the characteristics of the Sūrya images of south India, only by way of comparison. The south Indian sun-worship developed on indigenous lines; so there was hardly any impact of the East Iranian form of Sun-worship.[32] In the sun-images found in South India and several other places, there are no coats of mail, boots, Aruṇa, horses, halo and accessories. In place of halo there is a circle, and in place of coat there is Udarabandha. There are differences between the sun-images of North and South Indian traditions. According to G. Rao[33], "The

[31] Rao, Gopinatha, *Elements of Hindu Iconography,* Vol.I, Part II, p. 306ff.
[32] Sastri, H., *Iconography of South Indian Gods and Goddesses.*
[33] Rao, Gopinatha, *Elements of Hindu Iconography,* Vol.I, Part II, pp. 311-12.

South Indian figures of Sūrya have, as a rule, their hands lifted up as high as the shoulders and are made to hold lotus flowers only half blossomed; the images have the Udarabandha, their legs and feet are always left bare. The North Indian images, have generally their hands at the natural level of the hips or the elbows and carry full-blown lotuses, which rise upto the level of the shoulders, and their forelegs have coverings like socks, and the feet are protected with a pair of footwear resembling boots. The Udarabandha is not found in the northern variety of the images, but a thin cloth or a sort of coat or mail is shown as being worn on the body. The common features, of both the varieties (N & S) of Sūrya, are that the head is in all cases adorned with a Kiriṭa surrounded by a circular halo or prabhā-maṇḍala."

The features of the Sun-images, described by the North Indian texts are seen in the images of the Kusāṇa, Gupta and early medieval periods. There are many alien traits in them, such as Udīcyaveśa, Avyanga, *Pāde Upānhat,* etc. These alien traits emphasise, the foreign origin of northern variety of the Sun-cult introduced in India in the beginning of the Christian era or even much earlier[34].

NON-INDIAN FEATURES IN THE IMAGES OF SŪRYA

The legends that are current about the introduction of the form of Sun-worship, with the type of the anthropomorphic figure of the Sun-God as the cult picture, have been briefly referred so far. But certain details are worth considering.

The most important element is their Udīcyaveśa the dress of a northerner. It consists of a long heavy cloak covering practically the whole of the body and some sort of 'boots' or 'leggings'. This type of garment, though not in vogue among the Indians of ancient times, was much in use among the early foreign rulers of the śaka, Pahlava and Kuṣāna.[35] The headless inscribed statue of Mahārājādhirāja Devaputra Kaniṣka in the Mathura museum typifies this mode of dress. One of the earliest

---

[34] Banerjee, J.N., *Development of Hindu Iconography,* p. 437.

[35] Agarwala, V.S., *Harsh Carita,* p. 150ff suggests that special cloth for long coat was imported from Iran.

texts, alludings to this trait of the Sūrya figure, is the passage in the chapter of "Pratimā Lakṣaṇāni of the Bṛhatsaṁhitā.[36] It reads Kuryādudīcyaveśam gūḍham *Pādāduro Yāvat* means (the figure of the Sun-God) should be made with the dress of a notherner (the body) from the feet upwards to (the top of), the breast being hidden means "covered by a garment". It further characterises these images as "*Kundalabhūṣitavadanaḥ*" —"face adorned with ear-rings", "Viyadgavṛtaḥ" with a viyadga, viyanga or avyanga, the Indianised form of aiwiyaonghana, the sacred waistgirdle of the Iranians attached and *Kañcukaguptaḥ Smitaprasanna Mukhaḥ* his smiling pleasant face being covered partly by a cheek-plate. Scholars arrived at the conclusion, on the basis of unmistakable literary evidence, that a type of solar cult was introduced into India from Eastern Iran in the early centuries of the Christian era; the peculiar non-Indian features of Sūrya icons were long ago regarded as nothing but its archaeological corroborations. The Bṛhatsaṁhitā and many iconographic texts again emphasise such alien features of the Sūrya figures, as Udīcyaveśa (northern dress), avyanga the Indian form of the Iranian aiwiyaonghana, the sacred woollen waist girdle, which a Zoroastrian is enjoined to wear, etc. which are almost invariably present in the extant North-Indian specimens, these elements were, gradually subdued, and in later Sun images of Northern India, the covering of the upper part of the body was barely suggested by the artists, though their legs continued to be shown as encased in 'boots'. The nearest Indian analogy of the "Udīcyaveśa" which the ancient myth-makers of India could think of was the Kavaca, the protective coat of mail, which was well-known to them from a very early period.[37] In some later iconographic literature like the Viṣṇudharmottara (Khaṇḍa III, Ad. 67, verse 3), etc. the God is described as "covered with an armour" — Kavacenābhi saṁvṛtaḥ", though such terms as "Udīcyaveśa" and Yāviyānga" (this should be avyanga) are also

---

[36] Bṛhatsaṁhitā, Chap. 57, (verses 46-48).

[37] The Vedic description of Varuṇa who is described as wearing a golden coat of mail – "Bibhradrāpim hiraṇyayam varuṇa" (Rv. I-25, 13).

used in this connection. It is written as Udīcya veśas svākārassarvābharaṇa Saṁyutaḥ.... Kartavyā raśanā Cāsya yāviyangeti Samjñitā; (V.D. Ad. 67, Verses 2-3) it should be noted that Yāviyānga or Avyanga is rightly called here a raśanā or a waist-girdle.

As regards the peculiar dress of this Sun-God, one other interesting observation can be made here, namely, that we know of, at least, two other Indian deities who are ordered to be depicted as dressed in the northern fashion. Hemadri in his Vratakhaṇḍa[38], while describing the images of Chitragupta and Dhanada (Kubera), lays down that both of them are to be shown as dressed like a northerner and the latter is also to be endowed with a coat of mail (Kavacī)[39]. Chitragupta, who is to be placed on the right side of Yama, is to hold a pen in his right hand and a leaf in his left. Curiously enough, we see in the Chitragupta some interesting resemblances, as far as its iconography is concerned, with the pen and ink-pot carrying right-hand attendant of Sūrya who is known in iconographic literature by various names, such as Kuṇḍi, Piñgala, Dhātā, etc.

The elaborate legend about Sūrya's marrying Saṁjñā, the daughter of Viśvakarmā, her flight from his unbearable effulgence and Viśvakarmā's attempt at reducing the unendurable tejas of Sūrya, was composed to explain the peculiar foot-gear of the Sun-God. It is narrated that Viśvakarmā put the sun on his lathe (Śāna-yantra) and dimmed his brightness by peeling much of its from the upper part of his body, but he left his legs untouched[40]. So some texts[41] try to explain away this covering of

---

[38] Vol.II, 145-46.

[39] For sculptures of Kubera with his feet shod and his body well-covered with a tunic accompanied by his consort, Hariti. See Foucher, M., *Beginnings of Buddhist Art,* p. 145, pl. XVIII, 1-2.

[40] Pārśśva tu daksiṇa tasya citraguptam tu kārayet/ Udīcyaveśam svākāram dvibhujam saumyadarśanam/ Dakṣiṇe lekhanī tasya vāme patram tu kārayet/ Dhanadakartavyaḥ padmapatrābho varado naravāhanaḥ/ Cāmikarābhaḥ varadaḥ sarvabharaṇabhusitāḥ Lambodaraścaturbāhurvāmapingala locanaḥ/ Udīcyaveśa kavacī hāra bhārārdito haraḥ/

[41] Matsya Purāṇa, Ad. 261, verse 4, Bangiya Sāhitya Parishat Patrikā (Vol.XVI), Pandit B. Bidyavinod in his article on Sūrya-pade Upānhat (shoes on the feet of the Sūrya).

the legs as the sculptor's attempt at representing the tejas of the Sun as enjoined in the Matsya Purāṇa. This Purāṇa contains the interesting record that "It is only in some sculptures that the body (of the god) is shown covered with a garment consisting of two pieces of cloth, his feet being (really) covered by his effulgence" — "Colakacchanna vapuṣām Kvaciccitreṣu darśayet/ Vastrayugma Samopetam caraṇau tejasāvṛtau." Thus, the writers of such texts had in their view two different types of Sūrya figures, North Indian and South Indian.

Again, Sūrya's feet are covered simply by his brightness, but how is it that we find these self-same boots on the legs of his two male attendants Daṇḍa and Piñgala? One other interesting feature about these images, seem to have been noticed by very few scholars, viz. even that the legs of the female attendants of Sūrya in many reliefs[42] are covered by these identical boots. But the authors of these iconographic texts strictly enjoin that the legs of the Sun-God are on no account to be shown bare by the sculptor. Any sculptor violating this strong injunction will do so at the risk of becoming a leper for seven consecutive births. This story as well as those iconographic texts, which notice this peculiar feature of this type of Sūrya image shows clearly, in this case at least, that the types of the icons were evolved at first, and then rules were laid down in correspondence with the type already arrived at, for the future construction of such images. Gradually, this alien characteristic of the image of the Sun, was lost sight of and the South Indian sculptor had no fear of being afflicted with leprosy, when he carved the image of the Sun with his legs bare, long after the booted Sūrya was sculptured for the first time by his brother artists in Northern India.

Śrī Viśvakarmāvatāra Śāstra[43] describes the image of Sūrya thus: "The Sun-God should be placed on a divine one-wheeled chariot with seven horses driven by the charioteer who is no other than (Aruṇa) the younger brother of Tārkṣya. He should be

[42] Cf. those exhibited in the Gupta Gallery of the Calcutta Museum.

[43] See *Indian Antiquary*, Vol.LIV, 1925, p. 166, Śrī Viśvakarmāvatāra Śāstra, Chap. 28, verse 51-53.

wide-chested, red-coloured and beautiful like a water lily. A thousand brilliant rays should emanate from him and he should be adorned with jewelled ear-rings. The body of the image should be covered by a coat of mail. He should be adorned with jewelled ear-rings. He should hold two beautiful lotuses by their stalks and the lotus blossoms should be shown parallel to shoulders".[44]

Though no mention is made here of the Avestan waist-girdle — the avyanga and of the northern style of dress (Udīcyaveśa) which are as we have seen, mentioned in an earlier work, viz. the Bṛhatsaṁhitā (Chap. 58), still, wc do not fail to find a reference to the fact of the Sun's body being covered, evidently alluded to by Varāhamihira in the term "Gūḍham Pādāduro Yāvat".

"The texts noted above are of North-Indian origin; the only probable South-Indian text known to us referring to this feature, in a slightly different manner, is the Pūrvakāraṇāgama. A passage in its 13th section (Paṭala) as quoted by G. Rao describes the God as having his body covered with an armour (Kañcukāñcita Vigrahaṃ) but his feet are described as "(adorned) with a zone or girdle" (Pādau Śakaṭakau).[45]

One of the stories indirectly associated with the shoes on the divine feet may be found in the epic account of the introduction of the use of shoes among mankind for the first time. How shoes, made of (animal's) skin, were first represented to the sage Jamadagni alongwith an umbrella by the Sun-God in the guise of an old Brāhmin as protective devices against the burning rays of the Sun, is glibly told in the Mahābhārata.[46] But the connection of this account, with the main trait of the North Indian images of Sūrya, is not definite and clear.

The epic reference, however, to some peculiar physical features

---

[44] Śrī Viśvakarmāvatāra Śāstra, Chap. 28, verses 51-53.

[45] Rao, Gopinatha, *Elements of Hindu Iconography*, Vol.I, Part II, App.C, pp. 89-90. The text reads Sakhetakau which Rao corrects to Sakaṭakau; if the original reading is retained the passage would mean "The feet with shields" i.e. the shielded or the covered feet.

[46] MBH, Anuśāsana Parva, Ad. 95-96.

of Karṇa appears to have distinct bearing on it, and thus deserves special attention. The Mahābhārata refers on various occasions and contexts to the *Kavaca* and *Kuṇḍala,* adorned with which Karṇa was born to mother Kunti, before she was married to Pāṇḍu. Sūrya was invoked by her in her virgin state, to test the efficiancy of a mantra (Charm) received by her from Durvāsā, after having satisfied the dire sage with her untiring service, during his stay at her father's place. The God appeared before her and had a union with her in spite of her fears and wishes. When Karṇa was born to her in due course, he was found to have attached to his body a *Kavaca* and golden *Kuṇḍala* and to possess the bull-like shoulders and greenish yellow eyes of his father.[47] These inborn *Kavaca* and *Kuṇḍala* made Karṇa indestructible. The aforesaid details about Karṇa's life leave little doubt, that in him is to be found a fairly clear allusion to the particular trait of the Sūrya icons of the re-oriented Sun cult of Northern India. *Kavaca,* of course, stands for the close covering, the Udīcyaveśa — of Sūrya, but the significance of *Kuṇḍala* in this bearing is not very clear, it is meant to stand for an 'ear-ring': it is true that in the Bṛhatsaṁhitā, description of the Sun-icons, mention is made of it as a face ornament but so much stress is laid in this epic story on *Kuṇḍala* (this section is called Kuṇḍalā-haraṇa parva) the word seems to have some association with another of their alien traits. If it is understood in its original sense, which is something like a circular rope-coil, we may find here a reference to the *avyanga* of the texts noted above. It should be observed, however, that in the epic passages containing such references to *Kuṇḍala*, as we have seen them now, the word is used in the sense of an ear-ring. But, can it be regarded as a case of more common sense of a word influencing its less common one, and thus introducing the necessary change in the texts? In any case, the allusion to Karṇa's inborn, Kavaca is without doubt based upon Udīcyaveśa of the figures of his father.

A brief reference to the birth of Revanta, as given in the

---

[47] MBH, III. 307, 4-5.

Mārkaṇḍeya Purāṇa[48], will also enable us to recognise in his description a similar but indirect reference to it. "This son of Sūrya out of his union with his consort Saṁjñā in the shape of a mare in the Uttarakuru region was born holding a sword and bow clad in armour, riding on horseback and carrying arrows and quiver!"

The story of Sūrya and his two consorts, Saṁjñā and Chāyā (Saṁjñā's shadow-substitute), as narrated at length in the Purāṇa, lays stress in a very interesting manner on this particular trait of one class of the Sun-icons. The Bhaviṣya and Mārkaṇḍeya[49] Purāṇas among others give us in detail the story of the marriage of Sūrya with Saṁjñā, the daughter of Viśvakarmā. Her flight from him show that she could not bear the unendurable effulgence of her consort. So she left her shadow-form Chāyā with him as her substitute, in order that he might not notice her absence. Her flight was at first to her father's place and then to *Uttarakuru* where she performed austerities in the shape of a mare; at the union of Sūrya and Saṁjñā in the forms of a horse and a mare in Uttarakuru out of which the twingods the Aśvinas and Revanta were born.

There are two versions of the story in the Mārkaṇḍeya Purāṇa; in its second and more elaborate one a reference is made to the permission given to Viśvakarmā[50] by the Sun-God to trim and dim him. This incidental allusion indicates, in a subtle manner, the necessity of this account of explaining the change in the bodily features of the God. The couplet just preceding this verse seems also to allude to the most ancient Iranian and Indian modes of depicting the Sun-God by means of such symbols as a 'round disc' or 'a wheel'. It explains[51], "In as much as the Sun's form was formerly spherical, so the adorable Sun said to Tvaṣṭṛ "Be it so". But what is of special interest in this connection is

---

[48] Pargiter, F.E. (trans.), *Markaṇḍeya Purāṇa*, p. 576.

[49] Ibid., Chap. 57-58.

[50] Viśvakarmā Tvanujñātaḥ Śakadvīpe Vivasvataḥ/ Bhramimāropya tattejaḥ Śātanāyopacakrame//

[51] Yato hi bhāsvato rūpam prāgāsitparimaṇḍalam/ Tatastheti tām prāha tvaṣṭāram bhagavān raviḥ//

that the extensive mythology, summarised above, is nothing but an adaptation of the Vedic story about the marriage of Saraṇyu, the daughter of Tvaṣṭṛ with Vivasvanta the Sun-God. The original story of Saraṇyu's marriage occurs, as a brahmodya (a sort of riddle) in many of the Vedic texts.[52]

In brief, it appears to have been something like this: Tvaṣṭṛ instituted a marriage pagent for his daughter Saraṇyu; at this news all the people of this earth came together. Yama's mother (she became so, after her marriage), while being with mighty Vivasvant, disappeared. They hid away the immortal woman from the mortals, making Savarṇā ('a like one') as Chāyā or the 'shadow substitute' of the Puranic development. They gave her to Vivasvant. She bore him the Aśvinas who were abandoned by her.[53]

[52] Rv. I, 164, Av. X, 9-10.

[53] See for the Vedic myth Bloomfield's note on "the Marriage of Saraṇyu", Tvaṣṭṛ's daughter in *JAOS*, Vol.XVC, 1893, pp. 172-88.

FOUR

DESCRIPTION OF THE IMAGES OF SŪRYA

In the previous chapters, we have tried to give the references, as much as possible, of the Sun-God and his cult from Sanskrit literature. Now we propose to give here how far the descriptions given in literature confirm with the existing remains of the images of the Sun-God in various temples and museums.

We give here the description of some of the images, published as well as unpublished. The description of unpublished images are equally authentic and reliable because they are based on the descriptions in published works. We have tried to write in detail about the principal images, which we find in different books or catalogues. We have also given a table which gives the earlier classification of the images, some of which we have described.

SYMBOLS

It is clear that representation of the Sun-God in human form was preceded by symbolical representations on coins and seals.[1] It is only from the 5th cent. AD onwards, we start getting references to the regular images of the sun. This fact is directly expressed in the Sāmba Purāṇa[2], where it is stated that in ancient times there was no image of the sun. The Sun was worshipped by his devotees in early days in a circular form, just as there is the disc in the sky.

Gold-disc or the wheel: The symbol of the Sun-God in the Vedic literature, has been a Cakra.[3] This became one of the prominent emblems of Viṣṇu in the later mythologies[4].

Sometimes, a round golden-plate or a fire-brand stood for the

---

[1] *Journal of Indian Society of Oriental Art*, XVI, 51.

[2] Sāmba Purāṇa, 29.2 "*na purā pratimā hyāsit Pūjyate maṇḍale raviḥ*".

[3] Macdonell, *Vedic Mythology*, p. 155.

[4] Gonda, J., *Aspects of Early Viṣṇuism*, Utrecht, 1954, p. 96ff.

sun.[5] The earliest Indian coins, the punch-marked coins, bear on their face various peculiar figures which can certainly be taken, to symbolise the great celestial luminary.[6] A spoked wheel with other variants of the same figure, can be assumed easily, to stand for Buddhist Dharmacakra. It is very regularly found on these coins. This spoked wheel with its variants occurs also in the indigenous coins of Taxila and in many other coins.[7] The representation of the sun as "a rayed disc" occurs also on the early punch-marked coins and in the coins of the local rulers of Northern India.[8] Cunningham takes these spoked wheel symbols for Dharmacakra in some cases, but they can equally well be assumed to symbolise the sun himself, depending upon the period and area of the coin. Spooner[9] who was at first inclined to find in them Buddhist characteristics, subsequently abandoned his views about these marks and held the opinion that *they were all solar symbols,* though he would take them to be Zoroastrian in character. Again in certain places the "rayed disc of the Sun" is placed on an altar and surrounded by a railing, thus clearly indicating that the figures enclosed within the railing, were really objects of worship inside a shrine.[10] Cunningham always describes this figure as "rayed circle of sun on Buddhist basement railing", but there seems to be no good ground, as far as we can see, for describing this basement railing as Buddhist and it may equally well be taken to be Brahmanical in character.

Lotus: The lotus, originally, must have been the emblem designating the sun, but later, was utilised by the Buddhists for their own purposes. "On certain coins of the very earliest period,

[5] Śatapatha Brāhmaṇa, 7, 4, 1 — In piling the fire altar a disc of gold was placed on it to represent the Sun.

[6] Cunningham, *Coins of Ancient India,* p. 43. He traces the origin of the punch-marked coins to a period earlier than 1000 BC. However, the later researches indicate that even though they are the earliest, tracing them to 1000 BC requires much further work.

[7] Ibid., pl. III-13; IV-14, IV-15.

[8] Ibid., pl. III-14; IV-13, V-6, V-9, etc.

[9] Archaeological Survey of India, *Annual Reports,* 1905-06, pp. 150-55.

[10] Cunningham, *Coins of Ancient India,* pl. VII-6, 9, etc.

small ingots of silver and copper of a definite weight, are affixed a few marks, which look like very crude representations of a lotus. On other ancient coins too, certain symbols are to be found, which are nothing but attempts to figure the lotus flower intimately connected with the sun from the very earliest times."[11] Thus, the lotus flower is mentioned in the most ancient literature of the Indo-Āryans and it played a conspicuous part in the mythology of Brahmanism; its association with the sun was due to the fact that the opening and closing of the flower times with the rising and the setting of the sun.[12] This observation as regards the connection of the lotus flower with the sun is fully borne out by the evidence of the Pūraṇas, which enjoin the execution in sculpture of a twelve petalled lotus, because, there are twelve months in a year, and on different petals of which, figures of the different aspects of the Sun-God are to be placed with the God Bhāskara on the central pericarp[13] (Karṇikā). The lotus flower, as symbolising the Sun and representing other ideas or principles connected with the Sun[14], came to hold such a unique position in Indian Art of all ages and all religions that, in the portion of the Viṣṇudharmottara[15] dealing with iconographic matters, we find full and detailed instruction figuring of a lotus flower.

Thus, we have seen that in ancient Indian art, the Sun-God was represented by various forms and the like. When he came to be anthropomorphically represented, these wheel and lotus flower symbols were not totally discontinued and we know that

---

[11] *Indian Antiquary*, Vol.LIV, p. 162.

[12] Hastings, *Encyclopaedia of Religion and Ethics*, Vol.8, pp. 142-45.

[13] Hemadri in his Vratakhaṇḍa (pp. 528, 535 and 539), quotes from Bhāgavata Purāṇa, Skanda Purāṇa and Matsya Purāṇa, the respective passages dealing with Divākara Vratam, Āditya Vratam and Sūrya Naktavratam. See also p. 553, about Sūryavrata from Saura Dharma, "Upaliya sūcau deśe, sūryamtatra Samārcayet/ Samlikhet tatre Padmantu Dvādaśoram Sakarṇikam/ And red flowers (Rakta Puṣpa) were specially offered to Sūrya in his worship.

[14] Hastings, *Encyclopaedia of Religion and Ethics*, Vol.8, pp. 142-45. "Primarily, the lotus flower appears to have symbolised for the Aryans from very remote times, the idea of superhuman or divine birth and secondarily the creative force and immortality".

[15] Shah, Priyabala, Visnudharmottara, Vol.III, Chap. 45, verses 1-8.

the wheel (disc) and lotus were placed in the hands of Viṣṇu, one of the Ādityas and lotus flowers were placed in both the hands of the image of Sūrya himself. Moreover, the wheel and the lotus flower, as so many solar emblems, figured independently in many coins, seals, clay tablets and copperplate inscriptions of the Gupta period and afterwards.[16]

The twelve Ādityas are merged into one Sun-God under the name of Sūrya or Āditya. This emergence of sun in Āditya or Sūrya, as the 'Supreme' and original Sun-God, is a departure from the past and may be regarded as the epic innovation. The primary function of the Sun-God is to drive away darkness and demons.[17]

DESCRIPTIONS OF IMAGES (PUBLISHED)

The ornamentation, the clothing and the beautification of the images should be worked out in accordance with the usage in the country, in which the images are made. In India, images were made according to the rules laid down in the Śāstras. It may be noted that the Śāstras were written at different places and time, and therefore the variations in the iconography are found.

When images set up in the neighbourhood bestow prosperity and progress, it is thus required that, the outline of the faces and features and the details of clothing and ornamentation, should be made to vary from place to place according to local usage. In other respects no variation was allowed or encouraged. In any part of India, new canon of art other than the rules prescribed in the Āgamas and the Tantras are not found. These rules having been obeyed everywhere in the matter of making images.[18] It is no wonder, that the same results have been produced by artists belonging to all parts of the country, in so far as the art is apt to

---

[16] Fleet, *Gupta Inscriptions*, pp. 216, 269.

[17] MBH, III, 233, 8.

[18] See Shah, Priyabala, Viṣṇudharmottara, G.O.S., Baroda, Vol.II, p. 110, "An image made according to rules should be regarded excellent. It also tends to long life, fame and increase of riches. An image not observing the rules destroys riches. Gods should always be represented in beautiful images."

be bound down by rules. Thus, the Āgamas prescribe various proportions to the images of the various gods/goddesses. The proportions of the different parts and limbs of the body are given in the terms of Tāla. Tāla is said to be 12 angulas in extent.[19] An image, made according to rules, is looked upon as, blessing for the maker, the country and the king. Therefore, no effort should be spared in making it 'Salakṣaṇa'... This, in itself, is an aesthetic imperative. In the ancient tradition of India, beauty has always been associated with health, wealth and prosperity. In short, it is mangala.[20]

THE SCULPTURE OF BODHAGAYĀ[21]

In the Bodhagayā railing image (Ist cent. BC), the central figure represents the Sun (Sūrya) driving four-horsed chariot having one wheel (ekacakra) and attended on either side by a female figure each, rightly identified as Uṣā and Pratyuṣā, shoot at the Rākṣasas of darkness (Fig. 1).

The image of Sūrya at Bhājā *Vihara* (1st or 2nd cent BC)[22].

A.K. Coomaraswamy describes this image of Sūrya as a royal personage driving in a four-horsed chariot. He is accompanied by two women, one with Chatra (umbrella), the other a Chauri bearer. Figures on horse back form an escort. The chariot is being driven across the backs of very grossly proportioned nude female-demons, who seem to be floating face downwards in the air (Fig. 2). These nude female demons represent the demons of darkness and night. Coomaraswamy says that there is no reason to question the original identifications of this scene as representing Sūrya with his two wives driving through the sky and dispelling the powers of darkness. The Sun has been described as king of the heavenly world.

---

[19] Shah, Priyabala, Viṣṇudharmottara, G.O.S., Baroda, Vol.II, p. 106.
[20] Ibid., Vol.I, Ad. 38, Ślo. 24-27.
[21] Fergusson and Burgess, *The Caves and Temples of India,* p. 522.
[22] Coomaraswamy, A.K., *History of Indian and Indonesian Art*, fig. 24, p. 25.

MATHURĀ (KUṢĀṆA PERIOD — 2 CENT AD)

The Mathurā figure No. D.46[23], may be the earliest Mathurā figure, and that is from the Saptasamudrī well in Mathurā Museum. Here, the Sun-God wears a heavy tunic and is seated on a chariot drawn by four horses. He holds a lotus bud in his right hand and a broken dagger in the left. There are traces of top boots in his partially visible legs (Fig.3). He has Sun-disc or nimbus behind his head. Vogel (p. 105) remarks that it is, however, strange that a Vedic feature of the sun has been engrafted on an alien form (the Iranian features) of the deity.

The figure no. 269 (Fig.4) in the Mathura Museum depicts Sūrya as seated like a Kuṣāṇa emperor, wearing Indo-Scythian dress consisting of a tunic, trousers and plumpboots. The headdress is held fast by a chaplet and band. There are round earrings and a necklace round the neck.

Another figure, no. 513 in the Mathura Museum[24] represents a unique example of Piñgala, Sūrya's attendant holding a pen in right hand and an inkpot in the left, and clad in Kulah cap and Iranian coat. No. Dl in the same museum reflects the intercourse with the Pārasikas (Persians) is an important bust, which bears frizzled hair, a bearded chin, knotted scarf and cuirass. The bearded face reminds us of the description of the Persians given by Kālidāsa in his Raghuvaṁśa (IV-63), where the bearded faces of the Persians are compared to the bee-hives covered with black bees. Another important marked Sassanian feature on this image is the "Sun and Moon" symbol on the Kulaḥ cap.

Many images from Gāndhāra and Mathura regions of the Kuṣāṇa and the post-Kuṣāṇa periods (2nd cent. AD to 6th cent. AD) demonstrate the adoption of Iranian features such as high boots, northerner's dress, etc. Thus, there is a blending of the Hallenisitic, Indian and Iranian traditions.

---

[23] Vogel, *Catalogue of the Archaeological Museum at Mathura,* Allahabad, 1910, p. 104. See also Coomaraswamy, A.K., *History of Indian and Indonesian Art,* fig. 103, pp. 67-68.

[24] Agarwala, V.S., *Handbook of the Mathura Museum,* fig. 41, p. 52.

A figure of Sūrya (Fig. 5) in black stone, found in Gāndhāra (Kuṣāṇa period), is with high boots and a stooping figure beneath the chariot, reminds us of one of the demons of earlier sculptures. Except the high boots, other features, such as a chariot drawn by four horses and two female attendants on either side, are of the earlier tradition.

A beautiful image of Sūrya is carved on a lintel from Garhwa (Allahabad) (Fig. 6). The god is seated on a chariot drawn by four horses, with Aruṇa as the charioteer, and figures of Uṣā and Pratyuṣā on right and left respectively. The Sun-God has lotuses in both the hands. This image is of the Gupta period.

THE SŪRYA IMAGE FROM BHUMARĀ (NAGOD, MADHYA PRADESH) OF THE 6TH CENT. AD.[25]

Here, the Sun-God is standing and has two hands. There is a plain halo behind his head. He wears a tall cylindrical head-dress. In his left hand, he holds a lotus, while his right hand is damaged. The God wears long boots and a long coat tied at the waist with a sash. He is attended by two men who wear peculiarly long Scythian coats, tied with a belt and long boots. They also wear tall pointed conical caps like the Scythians. The figure on the right holds a lance or spear in his right hand, while that on the left holds a lotus. The horses of the Sun-God are absent.[26]

KUMBHĀRAVĀDĀ CAVE AT ELLORA

The whole front of this cave, which is next to the north must have been supported by six columns and pilasters. On the ceiling of the vestibule is a figure of Sūrya[27], the Sun-God in his chariot drawn by seven horses and Aruna with a female at each side shooting with a bow (Fig. 7).

From this to Cave XXVI (p. 40), which is known by the

[25] Banerjee, J.N., *Development of Hindu Iconography*, p. 436 assigns it to the Late Gupta period.

[26] Banerjee, R.D., *The Temple of Śiva at Bhumarā*, pl. XIVa.

[27] Fergusson and Burgess, *The Caves and Temples of India*, p. 444, pl. LXXXII, fig.2 and 8.

names of Kumbhāravādā and Sureśvara (at Ellora), the distance is about 70 yards. On the roof of the antechamber is the figure of Sūrya[28], the Sun-God in his chariot from which the temple derives the name of Sureśvara. The shrine door has a Dravidian moulding on the frieze and by the jambs are tall dvārapālas standing on lotuses with very bushy locks and long swords.

In India Museum at Calcutta[29], there is a Sūrya image which bears an inscription in proto-Bengali characters on the pedestal which reads as follows:

Om Śrīmad Vaktraśivāchārya Kārito bhāti Kāṁadaḥ/
Sūryaḥ Samastarogāṇāṁ harttā Viśvaprakāśakaḥ//

The translation goes like this:

"This image of the sun who bestows splendour and fulfils desires, removes all diseases and illumines the universe, has been made by the master Vaktraśiva." This figure, probably, should be relegated to the end of the 11th or the beginning of the 12th century.

As in the case of all South Indian images of this God, the hands of Sūrya are, in this instance also lifted upto the level of the shoulders and carry a lotus flower each. On the right and left of Sūrya are Uṣā and Pratyuṣā driving away the darkness before them with their bows and arrows. Here the chariot of Sūrya has two wheels instead of only one, as required by the Sanskrit authorities. This sculpture may be designated to the eighth century.

In the Śiva temple at Melcheri, near Kāveri-pākkam, there is an image of Sūrya which belongs to the later Pallava period (AD 800). Here, the Sun-God is standing upon a flat seat under which are the seven horses are carved with the driver Aruṇa. This is a fine piece of sculpture similar to the one found in Ellora.

Khajuraho temple-complex has also supplied Sun-images of two varieties — the seated and the standing.

In the Citragupta Temple of Khajuraho[30], we get a very good

---

[28] Burgess, J., *The Caves of Ellora and Other Brahmanical and Jain Caves in Western India*, p. 40.

[29] Archaeological Survey of India, *Annual Reports*, 1930-34, p. 257.

[30] Awasthi, R.A., *Khajuraho ki Deva Pratimayen*, p. 172.

standing variety of Sun-images. In this sculpture, the sun wears Kiriṭa Mukuṭa, Kuṇḍala, garland, Yajñopavīta (the sacred thread) and aviyanga. He has a halo round his head. He has high boots. He has Daṇḍa and Piñgala on his left and right side. There are attendant dieties as Aśvins, two queens, Aruṇa and perhaps Pṛthvī. There are seven horses also.

Another image of the seated form of Sūrya, from Śiva temples (Duladeo, Khajuraho) of the 10th cent. AD.[31] is very interesting. The figure has eight arms. Some of the arms are broken. He is covered with a coat of mail, it has dwindled into a strip underneath the ornaments of his chest and extends to the belt. He is seated with his feet locked in Padmāsana, a long cloth covers them to the heels. This costume indicates that the consuming power of Sūrya's body is covered. In earlier images (from Mathura etc.) the body of Sūrya is completely covered with a coat of mail, high boots and other accoutrement of the dress of northerners who had brought this particular cult to India. This figure is overlaid by heavy ornaments, arms and weapons. In his two hands, Sūrya holds full blown lotus flowers, symbols of manifestation of time; this aspect is also upheld by Śiva holding in his right hand a Triśūla, the trident — where past, present and future meet in one point, while serpents in the left hand are amongst the ornaments of Śiva; here they strengthen, in the opposition of their nature to that of the sun, the total symbolism (cf. Sun-bird and serpent) of the image. The hands of Brahmā hold the rosary, the cycle of time and its resorption and the Kamaṇḍalu. But for the trident no other weapons are seen now in the hands of the image. The hands of Viṣṇu might have held the disc and the club. The weapons held in the hands of the images of the gods, represent portions of the unbearable power of the Sun, which Viśvakarman had sliced away from it. Viśvakarman made the disc of Viṣṇu, the trident for Śiva and other weapons for these and the other gods out of the particles of power that he took away from the Sun (cf. Matsya Purāṇa, XI 27-30).

[31] Kramrisch, Stella, *The Hindu Temples*, pl.VI, pp. 373-74.

This image of Sūrya, the Sun-God would embrace Brahmā, the presiding divinity of the Sun; Viṣṇu, the presiding divinity of Moon; and Śiva who presides over the Fire[32]. Such an image is a support of a meditation on Sadāśiva and has its place of special importance in a temple of Śiva.

The small mutilated image of Aruṇa, in the centre of the drapery, near the edge of the pedestal, lies in the vertical axis by which the Kīrtimukha in the crown of Sūrya is linked to the three horses carved on the pedestal, the seat of the chariot of the Sun-God.

The image of Sūrya on pl. LXXXVI appears to be the oldest among those whose illustrations are published in this book[33]. It belongs to the Paraśurāmeśvara temple at Gudimallam in Tamil Nadu. It has its hands lifted up to the level of the shoulders and from the features of the face and the peculiarities of the modelling in general, this image may well be taken to belong to a period anterior to the 7th cent. AD. He stands bare-footed on a pedestal on which his horses are not shown. The upper part of the body is left bare. The hands of the god raised to the level of the shoulders, hold two lotus buds (Fig. 8). There is another sculpture of the 8th century. This is the seated figure of Sūrya whose photograph is produced on pl. LXXXIX in EHI. In this sculpture, Sūrya is seated cross-legged in his chariot drawn by seven horses driven by Aruṇa. Around him are to be seen the figures of the Goddesses Rājñī, Suvarṇā, Suvarchasā and Chāyā as also the figures of Daṇḍa and Piñgala. The photographs reproduced on pl. XC are interesting and represent the North Indian type of the image of the Sun-God. The images of Sūrya, illustrated in this book, wear a curiously shaped Kiriṭamakuṭa with a flat top and have the characteristic round face associated with North Indian sculptures. Their hands are placed at the level of the hip, and a lotus with a long stalk is held in each of them, the flower itself being at the level of the shoulders. In the Elements of Hindu

---

[32] Iśānaśivagurudeva Paddhati III, Chap. XII, pp. 27-29.
[33] Rao, Gopinatha, *Elements of Hindu Iconography*, Vol.I.

Iconography (Figs. 1 & 2), the Goddesses Rājñī and Nikṣubhā are seen on the extreme right and left of Sūrya, while nearer him on either side are Daṇḍa and Piñgala. In Fig. 1, the Aśvini-Devatās with horse-faces are shown seated in small niches, specifically provided for them, whereas in Fig. 2, the figures of Uṣā and Pratyuṣā are seen, as if engaged in chasing darkness with their bows and arrows. Below these are seen the some what damaged figures of the Goddesses Rājñī and Nikṣubhā; and immediately below the feet of Sūrya are worked out the seven horses of the Sun-God's chariot. The images of Sūrya in (Figs. 1 & 2), on this plate, have a broad belt round their waist which is perhaps the avyanga or ahyanga mentioned in the Bhaviṣya Purāṇa. Fig. 3, contains the central image of Sūrya and surrounding it are the images, of Daṇḍa and Piñgala and the horse-faced Aśvini-Devatās as also Uṣā and Pratyuṣā, the latter are as usual chasing away darkness with their bows and arrows and are sculptured near the Kāntimaṇḍala of Sūrya. The body of Sūrya is shown as covered with a thin fabric, through which his body is clearly visible. The avyanga in this figure is not a broad band, but a narrow belt encircling the waist. The three figures on this plate are seen wearing socks and boots. The photograph reproduced on the pls. XCI & XCII are of Sūrya of the South Indian variety belonging to the Chalukya — Hoyaṣalā country. The hands of Sūrya in these cases are lifted upto the level of the shoulders and are found to carry half-blown lotuses. There are the udarabandha and the avyanga but no sort of footwear. In pl. XCI the Goddesses Rājñī and Nikṣubhā are depicted as standing one on each side of Sūrya with a chāmara in their hands. This description agrees with the description given in Agni Purāṇa (Ad. 51). In pl. XCII the Goddesses Uṣā and Pratyuṣā are as usual driving away darkness with bows and arrows. Besides these, a number of small figures are covered probably to represent Daṇḍa and Piñgala and others. On the topmost tier of the sculpture stand five figures, resembling boys, these are perhaps the Ṛṣis Sanaka and others. In the tier below this first one, are a set of musicians playing upon different musical instruments. In pl. XCI & XCII are seven horses, but in the next figure of Aruṇa is shown. Fig. 1, pl. XCIII and Figs. 1 & 2 on pl. XCIV also belong to the South Indian variety of Sūrya and to Tamil Nadu. In these the absence of the attendant deities may be noticed; these images except Fig. 1, pl. XCIV, wear Udarabandha and Avyanga, the figures of the seven horses carved below the seat of the Sūrya are not seen in the remaining images. Fig. 1, pl. LXXXVIII is the reproduction of the photograph of a bronze statuette of Sūrya preserved in the Madras Museum. In this, Sūrya is seen seated upon a chariot having a single wheel drawn by seven horses and driven by Aruṇa. This figure is encircled by a Prabhāvalī. The Goddesses Rājñī waving a Chāmara and Nikṣubhā with what appears to be an umbrella are seen standing on either side of Sūrya. Fig. 2 on the same plate is a piece of sculpture belonging to the modern Bombay School. It is carved in marble, Sūrya is here shown with four hands carrying a lotus each in the back hands and the Akshamālā and the Kamaṇḍalu in the front ones, and seated upon a chariot drawn by seven horses driven by Aruṇa. Fig. 2, pl. XCIII belongs to the North Indian variety; the figure of Sūrya has a face belonging to the pan-type. Strangely enough, it is seen holding the hands as high as its shoulders and the lotuses carried in them are at the higher level than the shoulders. Near the legs of the image of Sūrya are those of Daṇḍa and Piñgala and the Goddesses Rājñī and Nikṣubhā and one other between the legs of Sūrya. It is difficult to say whom this figure is meant to represent. Fig. 1, pl. XCIV belongs to the Hoyaśala country, the image of Sūrya has in this instance four hands, two in front in which are the lotuses and the back ones are seen carrying the Cakra and the Śankha. The seven horses and Aruṇa are sculptured below the foot of Sūrya. Pl. XCV represents the toraṇa or gateway of a Sūrya temple. On the columns and the archway of this toraṇa are sculptured the figures of eleven Ādityas, which together with the one in the central shrine make up the usual number of twelve Ādityas. Some of the Ādityas have two, other four goddesses attending upon them; each one is enshrined in a small fane and are seen carrying lotuses in their hands. All except the central figure on the archway are standing; the central figure is seated in a chariot to which are yoked the seven horses, characteristic of Sūrya. In the niches below the two Ādityas on either side of the central one are some figures, whose significance is not known.

From the study of these photographs of the images reproduced in the *Elements of Hindu Iconography*[34] (Vol.I, Part II) on pls. LXXXVI to XCIV, it may be seen clearly that there are two varieties among these images, viz. the North Indian and the South Indian. Each of these possesses very remarkable peculiarities which are easy to recognise.

The North Indian images have generally their hands at the natural level of the hips or the elbows and are made to carry full-blown lotuses which rise up to the level of the shoulders and their forelegs have coverings. The feet are protected with a pair of foot-wear resembling boots. The udarabandha is not found in the northern variety of the images of the Sun-God, but there is a thin cloth or a sort of coat of mail shown as being worn on the body.

The South Indian images of Sūrya, on the other hand, have, as a rule their hands lifted up as high as the shoulders and are made to hold lotus flowers, which are only half blossomed, the images have invariably the udarabandha and their legs and feet are always left bare. These images of Sūrya are usually with the seven horses and with or without their driver Aruṇa. Those which belong to the extreme south of South India, to such parts as the Tamil districts, do not possess any attendant deities like Daṇḍa, Piñgala and the goddesses. The images of the Sun-God as found in the Karṇāṭadeśa and the Southern Maharashtra country. Corresponding roughly to the ancient Çālukyas and Hoyaśalā kingdoms have invariably two goddesses sculptured one on each side of Sūrya.

The common features, of both northern and southern varieties of Sūrya, are that the head is in all cases adorned with a

[34] Rao, Gopinatha, *Elements of Hindu Iconography,* Vol.I, Part II.

Kiriṭa surrounded by a circular halo or Prabhā Maṇḍala and that in several instances the characteristic seven horses and their charioteer Aruṇa are not missing.

At Hansi in Punjab[35] there are many Hindu and Buddhist monuments, but the most valuable of these sculptures is a standing image of the Sun-God, which from the iconographical point of view, is one of the best examples yet found in Northern India. The main point of interest is the accuracy with which the artist has followed the description of the Sūrya image as given in the Śāstras. The only difference is the absence of the one-wheeled chariot, the horses and Aruṇa. The height prescribed for images of the Sun is one, two, three or more cubits, each variety having its own special name. Similarly, in conformity with the Śāstric injunctions, the deity wears a Kiriṭa, a necklace over his chest, a Yajñopavīta and a girdle. It should be noted, however, that the hands of the deity which hold lotuses do not reach upto the level of the shoulders as is laid down in the Sādhanās. On either side of the main figure, on the same base, stand three figures. Among these, the figures standing next to the deity, are males holding a pen with folio and a spear (Sk. Śakti) respectively. They must, therefore, be Piñgala (Agni) and Daṇḍa or Daṇḍanāyaka (i.e. Skanda), who were posted on the right and the left sides of Sūrya by the gods to protect him from the attacks of Asuras. Sometimes, as in the image of the sun, at the sun temple at Konarak, these attendants hold a sword and a shield. The two females, exterior to Piñgala and Daṇḍa, are two of the four Śaktis of Sūrya, while the horse-headed male figures carved at the extreme ends are the Aśvini Devatās which according to the Bhaviṣya Purāṇa, have to be shown on either side of the deity. Higher up on both sides of Sūrya are the females Uṣā and Pratyuṣā who are chasing away the darkness with their bows and arrows. Above them we notice a seated figure on either side of Sūrya. The figure on the proper right side holds a Khaṭvānga in the right hand and might

[35] Archaeological Survey of India, *Annual Reports 1922-23*, pp. 92-93, pl. V, fig.1.

represent a form of Śiva. The seated figures, which are partly concealed by the lotuses of Sūrya, are of course Brahmā and Viṣṇu as distinguished by their respective symbols. A feature of this image, which is not generally met with in statues of the sun, is the representation of the nine planets along with the halo, the central figures being the Sun-God himself. The only writing on the statue is a short Nāgarī inscription, engraved on the folio in the left hand of Piñgala, which may possibly be read as *Śrī Āditya-Pratīmā.*

The remaining images found at Hansi include another representation of the sun which, however, is inferior in technique and omits the Aśvinikumāras noticed in the image described above. The figure seated between the knees of the main deity is probably meant for the legless Aruṇa.

MOḌHERĀ

The images of Moḍherā temple have long boots, in some cases, marked with lines crossing each other diagonally as if intended to represent impressed leather. In some cases the seven horses are represented below him, in others they are not.[36] Here (Fig. 9) is a standing image of Sūrya. He holds full-blown lotuses in his two hands, but hands are broken. He is well ornamented with a kiriṭa mukuṭa, kuṇḍalas, hāras, an armour covering the chest and a girdle-avyanga and also with udarabandha. He wears dhotī and boots. His uttarīya vastra is in the shape of a long garland. He is driven by seven horses. Below on the right and left are Daṇḍa and Piñgala in a seated position. Behind each of these attendants are Aśvinas the horse-faced gods. On both the sides of his head two gandharvās are seen with the garlands. While (in Fig. 10), Sūrya is accompanied by two male figures Daṇḍa and Piñgala holding Daṇḍa and pen and inkpot respectively. Here, attendants are standing on both the sides of his head, there are two small figures, perhaps gandharvās with the

---

[36] Burgess and Cousens, *Archaeological Survey of Western Gujarat* (Northern Gujarat), Vol.IX, 1902, p. 71.

Abhaya hastas. He is dressed and ornamented as usual, that is similar to Fig. 9. But the lotuses are above the shoulders; on the boots there are lines crossing each other diagonally. Here there are no horses, but the figure stands on a lotus.

The shrine is now in ruins, nothing but the bare walls remain. On clearing out the débris, the seat of the image of Sūrya was found in the middle of the floor, with other blocks connecting it with the side walls. On the front of the seat are carved the seven horses (The Saptāśva Vāhana) of the God. The doorway of the shrine is richly decorated and the figure of Sūrya is repeated over and over again, but the central block on the lintel where the dedicatory image, or some closely associated figure, is always represented, has been destroyed. There were no windows in the shrine walls here, their places would be occupied by the chief images, but in this instance the large niches on each side of the three windows contain the standing figures of Sūrya, each with his seven horses carved under his feet and perhaps his wives beside him.

Figures of Sūrya or Āditya occur everywhere on the architraves of the door jambs. There are twelve figures of Āditya in six large niches round the walls of the Pradaksiṇā Patha in the shrine and also six in the Maṇḍapa. Moreover, twelve images are on the exterior of the shrine walls. Usually he is represented with only two arms but as they projected forwards, they have mostly broken off. The other superhuman figures on the walls are generally distinguished by four arms each... The age of the temple may be inferred from its style to belong to about the 11th century or the reign of Bhīmadeva I (AD 1022–63). Now Cousens found, on one of the blocks forming the back wall in the shrine, a date inscribed but upside down and reading "Vikram Saṁvat 1083" i.e. AD 1026–27.

The extensive popularity of Sun-cult in Gujarat is shown by a number of Sun-images, found from the different parts of the country, and Sūrya tīrthas noted in Purāṇas. The standing figure, found at *Karvan* is, an excellent one and can easily be assigned to the 9th cent. AD at the latest. The Sūrya holds the lotus. It wears an ekāvalī, beaded armlets and a golden-chained girdle, with a chain hanging on each thigh. The oblong halo with a lotus petal-border on its circumference is remarkable. It has two small figures of Daṇḍa and Piñgala on both sides.[37]

The figures of the Sun-God found from Unza,[38] Roda[39] (13.5 kms. east of Himatnagar) and Ranu-pipli[40] (Pādrā tālukā, Dist. Baroda) are some of the good specimens of the seated posture. The image of *Ranu-pipli* is of 9th cent. AD. It is a good specimen. It is about 3.5 ft. high and 2 ft. broad. His one-wheeled chariot, ornamented with lotus-petals, is drawn by seven horses, with the forelegs raised, suggesting to be in action. Aruṇa is seated in the centre with two sets of reins held in the left hand. Uṣā and Pratyuṣā stand on the right and left side of the deity. The loose skirts of these two goddesses are shown floating in the air, because the chariot is in motion. Two male figures Daṇḍa and Piñgala are also shown. Sūrya is with a halo which is supported by a makara-toraṇa with two rows of lotus-petals. Sūrya has Kiriṭa Mukuṭa. His face is oval and eyes are in dhyāna-mudrā. He wears very elegant round Kuṇḍalas. He has Yajñopavita hanging down from the left shoulder. Of the two hands, the left holds a lotus-stalk and right one is broken. The deity is seated cross-legged in Padmāsana. The legs are covered with a semi-transparent cloth and not by the usual boots. The sculpture is assignable to the Pratihāra period i.e. not later than the 9th cent. AD.

In Gujarat, the temples began to be dedicted to the combined images of Viṣṇu and Sūrya, under the name of Sūrya Nārāyaṇa. A temple of Sūrya Nārāyaṇa was noticed by Burgess[41] at Somanatha (known as Prabhāsa) in Saurāṣṭra. This figure cannot be earlier than the 8th cent. AD. One temple dedicated to Sūrya Nārāyaṇa at Bhīmanātha has also been mentioned by Burgess.[42]

---

[37] *Journal of Gujarat Research Society*, April 1949, pls. LXVII-B, LXVIII-A, LXVIII-C and XLVIII-B.

[38] Ibid.

[39] Ibid.

[40] Ibid.

[41] Archaeological Survey of India, Vol. IX, p. 75.

[42] Ibid., p. 73.

Sūrya Nārāyaṇa (Prabhāsa) is seated in Padmāsana on a chariot. The Chief-God is Sūrya, represented here by his seven horses driven by a small-sized charioteer seated in front of the figure. The figure has three faces (Trimūrti). The main figure seems to have worn an udarbandha and a girdle. There is Prabhāmaṇḍala (halo) behind the head. The figure has six hands with dhyāna mudrā, two each for the three forms of Brahmā, Viṣṇu and Maheśa, which are broken. No emblems of the deities are seen. Yet enough remains to show that Sūrya was the main deity and was worshipped in this region along with other gods like Viṣṇu, Śiva and Brahmā. Thus, it is a Trimūrti with Sūrya (Viṣṇu) in the middle, the lotus-stalks being visible[43]. So, there may have been a temple at Prabhāsa[44], dedicated to this Trimūrti image. A similar Trimūrti image has also been preserved in a niche, in the shrine of Limboji Mātā at Delmāl.[45]

The seated figure of Sūrya with a beautiful round face from Unza belongs to this period; as it has all the artistic characteristics and stylistic affinities of the pre-Solanki sculptures. It is without prabhāmandala. The rosette-frame round the sculpture is noteworthy.

STANDING SŪRYA, MOUNT ABU (VAṢIṢṬHĀŚRAMA)

A two-armed standing Sūrya image is located at Vaṣiṣṭhāśrama, Mount Abu[46]. It is probably of 9th cent. AD. Here, the forms of female attendant are common, in the art of the Gurjara Pratihāra period in Western India. The double neck-ornament and the necklace with bell-design are noteworthy.

Rarely, we find from Gujarat, the sculptures of the seated Sūrya. The panel on the door-frame of the Varāha temple at Kadvār (near Somanath), assigned to the 8th century AD has an image of Sūrya, first from the right. It is seated on a lotus in the Utkaṭika (raised hips) pose and seems to have only two hands,

---

[43] Sankalia, H.D., *The Archaeology of Gujarat,* fig. 74, p. 162.
[44] Ibid.
[45] Ibid., fig. 73, p. 163-64.
[46] Majumdar, M.R., *Chronology of Gujarat*, p. 273.

which bear a lotus each, held as high as the shoulder. On a stone door-frame (12th century), at the Jūnagadha Museum, in a niche on the arch of the torana is found a seated Sūrya, in a chariot drawn by seven horses.

"Seated, yet headless, Sūrya images from Roḍa[47], about 9 miles east of Himatnagar, in the Old Idar State (now in Baroda 'Open Air Sculpture Gallery') are assigned to the late 9th century, roughly to the pre-Solanki period. The composite sculpture when complete, must have been a superb specimen of Indian Art. The modelling, the configuration, the balance and the proportions can be clearly discerned even from its mutilated condition"

SUN IMAGE AT SARKHEJ (AHMEDABAD DIST.)[48]

There is a remarkable Sun-image in the temple of Sarkhej village. This figure is the bust of Sūrya. He wears Kiriṭa. This image has two hands. In the hands, the god holds full-blown lotus. The lotus is up to the level of the shoulders. Above the lotus on each side is a figure of Aśvini Devatā (having the face of a horse). The God has a plain but circular halo or lotus or Prabhā-maṇḍala behind his head. He wears a circular kuṇḍalas of lotus and necklaces. On the left shoulder there is a upavīta and also he has girdle or kaṭibandha. Here the image is without attendants. This image of the Sun-God belongs to the 11th century AD. (Fig. 11)

In Gujarat, the consort of Sūrya and his son Revanta[49] are worshipped. The consort of Sūrya is popularly known as Rannādevī. She was worshipped at Rander (a place named after her on the right bank of river Tapti) and also at Daḍavā (Saurāṣṭra). Here, even now, come many devotees expecting to be blessed with children.[50]

Images of the consorts of Sūrya are in the Watson Museum, Rajkot and at Ḍhānk (Saurāṣṭra)[51]. This Rajkot image is of marble. The goddess has two hands and is in Samabhanga pose.

---

[47] Chhabra, B., *Baroda Museum Bulletin*, Vol.XII, 1955-56.
[48] Hazarnavisa, Ravi, Svādhyāya, pp. 199-200.
[49] Sankalia, H.D., *The Archaeology of Gujarat*, p. 214.
[50] See *Sūrya mandir Viśeṣāṅka*, p. 166.
[51] Sankalia, H.D., *The Archaeology of Gujarat*, p. 159.

Behind the head, there is a circular lotus-prabhā. On her either side is a female, chāmara-bearer.

The worship of the Navagrahas was in vogue also. They are carved usually with Sūrya on the doorway of the entrance and sometimes on the toraṇa of a Sūrya-image. All the Navagrahas are beautifully sculptured[52] on the outer door-frame of the Sūrya Mandira at Thān. The Sūrya toraṇas are at Piludrā (Mehsana Dist.). In this mutilated architrave there is a seated image of Sūrya with the lotus in the right hand. This seems a fragment of an old Sūrya temple. Moreover, similar toraṇas have been discovered from Vaḍnagar, Siddhapur, Kapaḍvanj and Pālanpur. From Siddhapur, a sun-image has been discovered.

THE TEMPLES OF BHUVANEŚWARA[53]

THE TEMPLE OF LINGARĀJA

On the right hand of the balustraded window of the eastern face is carved in a panel, a ratha (chariot) containing the figure of the Sun-God with four horses and Aruṇa, the charioteer. The representation of four horses, instead of seven, is most peculiar. The only instance of the Sun-God driving a four-horsed chariot is noticed in a bas-relief of a pillar at Bodhagaya regarding which, General Cunningham writes as follows — "In this treatment, I think, that, there is a decided evidence of Greek influence in the restricted number of the four horses attached to the chariot, for the Indian Sūrya, from the earliest times down to the present day, has always been represented as driving a chariot with seven horses. In the Rigveda he drives "Seven bay or bright-backed steeds" and in all Brahmanical sculptures that I have seen there are seven horses carved on the pedestal, which are being driven by Aruna while two attendants on each side shoot downwards the golden arrows of the solar rays."

---

[52] *Bombay Gazeteer*, Vol.XVI, p. 634.

[53] Ganguly, *Orissa and Her Remains*, p. 365.

THE TEMPLE OF DHARMARĀJA OR SŪRYA NĀRĀYAṆA[54]

Here the figure of Nārāyaṇa stands on a pedestal of stone carved with the figures of seven horses. This is evidently the figure of the sun or Sūrya Nārāyaṇa. The figures of the sun and Moon and Nārāyaṇa have been imported from Konaraka. There were originally figures of seven horses representing those for driving the chariot of the Sun-God.[55]

There are three huge figures of Sūrya or the Sun-God noticeable in the niches of the Vimāna, which are the roofs of three structures below the level of the figures of the Sun-God. The statue in the central niches of the north face represents the heroic figure of the Sun-God, seated on a nicely decorated horse, provided with a saddle showing the pommel and cantle distinctly.

The deity is kilted. The stone block out of which, the figure has been carved, has been oxidised badly. The figure of Aruṇa, the legless charioteer of the deity, with his seven horses is not noticeable here. The statue is flanked by two male figures having their hands broken, and judging from what still remains of the two figures, it is apparent that they were armed with a sword and shield, with two studs and a coat of arms in the centre. There are two tiny bearded figures standing between the two above statuettes and the Sun-God. There are the figures of the four-headed Brahmā and four handed Viṣṇu on the left and right respectively, both being seated on lotus pedestals. There are female figures, noticeable at the top of the trefoiled arch, playing on various musical instruments such as flute, viṇā, drums, cymbals, etc. Over these are seen, the flying nymphs carrying human figures and holding garlands. The trefoiled arch is surmounted at the top by a Kīrtimukha, flanked by two, male figures blowing conch shells.

In the central niche of the south face, there is a huge chlorite statue of Sūrya. The figure of the Sun-God is kilted and has the characteristic ornaments for the arm, neck and ear; and it has also a peculiar head-dress, the waist band has a central stud and

---

[54] Ganguly, *Orissa and Her Remains*, p. 428-29.
[55] Ibid., p. 447-48.

is provided with beaded tassels hanging down from it. The piece of cloth, worn by the deity reaching up to the knee, is exquisitely carved. There is a dagger on the pedestal on the left side. The hands of the statue are broken, they used to carry two full-blown lotuses, one of which still exists in the left. The pedestal of the statue is nicely carved with panels separated by thin beaded pillars; these panels contain groups of female figures, some playing on musical instruments and others dancing in a peculiar gait. The pedestal is also carved with the figures of seven horses driven by Aruṇa, the charioteer of the Sun-God sitting in front near the feet of the statue. The reins of the horses are exquisitely beautiful. Out of the two standing figures, the right one holds a sword and shield and the left one, a bow. The figures of Brahmā and Viṣṇu are noticed here also as in the case of the statue in the northern circle.

In the central niches of the western face[56], is seen a huge chlorite statue of Sūrya wearing kilts or boots reaching a little below the knee-cap. The figure has the conventional long ears with pendulous ear-rings, characteristic armlets, etc. The piece of cloth worn by the deity is nicely carved. The statue stands on a pedestal, the face of which is carved with the figures of horses. Aruṇa does not exist. The carvings and workmanship are similar to those in the niches on the north and the south[57].

KONARAKA

There is a beautiful dancing hall in front of the temple (The Black Pagoda at Konaraka). Here, a chlorite slab bearing a finely carved image of the Sun-God[58] is represented, standing under a trefoil arch (Fig.12). His two hands, holding lotus flowers, are broken. His eyes are unfinished. In front of him sits his charioteer, grasping with his left hand the reins of the seven horses, represented along the pedestal, and holding a whip in his right

[56] Ganguly, *Orissa and Her Remains*, p. 450.
[57] Ibid., p. 449.
[58] Archaeological Survey of India, *Annual Reports 1903-04*, pl. XXII-B, p. 46.

hand. On each side of the God, stands a male holding a shield and sword, and reminds one, somewhat, of the statues of the two warriors leading horses in front of the southern gate of the Maṇḍapa. Between the sword-bearers and the God are two small bearded Ṛṣis. Above, on small ornamented roofs, stand two females and at the bottom of the arch is a small figure of a man on horseback and a seated male playing upon a vīṇā or lute. The top of the arch is crowned by Kīrtimukha and on each side is a flying Gandharva holding garlands.

Neither the image nor the Vedi now stands at the place for which it was originally intended. It has been pointed out by Rai Prasanna Kumar Pal Bahadur, Honorary Assistant Engineer, that the eyes of the God having been left unfinished shows that the statue was never consecrated[59].... The statue seems to represent Aruṇa, the forerider of the rising Sun.

Here the temple[60] was fashioned to represent the twenty-four wheeled chariot of the Sun-God being drawn by seven horses. The wheels and the horses of the Sun-God's chariot rest on his stylobate, which forms a kind of a pedestal for the high ornamental plinth of the temple... and above this is another set of panels containing human figures, in revoltingly obscene postures.[61]

The wheels of the chariot temple are 9'9" in diameter, with eight wide and eight narrow spokes in each. Only a few of the wheels are now intact. The horses are all 4'9" high and have elaborately ornamented harness. They are built-up of a number of small dressed stones and not carved out of large blocks.

---

[59] Cousens suggests that it may have been intended to add silver plate eyes, as is so common a practice with images. Archaeological Survey of India, *Annual Reports*, pl. XXII-A.

[60] Kuraisi, Archaeological Survey of India, *New Imperial Series*, 1931, Vol.LI. (List of ancient monuments in the Provinces of Bihar and Orissa), p. 285.

[61] Bloch's remarks on these obscene figures are interesting. "The walls of the temple seem to have been carved," he says, "With the profusest illustrations in stone of the "Kama Sutra" that can be imagined. Whether this was done in order to drive away evil influences or to attract the people, I am unable to say. At present one hears both explanations in regard to similar carvings on temple walls and very likely both are true."

On the face of the architrave figures of the nine planets (Navagrahas) were carved. Of the Navagraha stone architraves, only one that form the eastern doorway, is now extant...... The figures are richly ornamented; wear high pointed crowns and are seated cross-legged on lotuses.[62] The first figure beginning from the left is that of *Ravi* or the *Sun*, holding a lotus in each hand, the second is that of *Soma* or the Moon, holding a vase in the left hand and a rosary in the right, the third figure is *Mañgala* (Mars), the fourth *Budha* (Mercury), the fifth *Bṛhaspati* (Jupiter), the sixth *Śukra* (Venus) and the seventh *Śani* (Saturn). All the figures are similar in form, features, ornaments, etc. except that of Jupiter, who, as priest of gods and sages, is depicted with a long flowing beard. The eighth figure is that of Rāhu or the ascending node, who is believed to have been produced by one human body being divided into two, the upper half forming Rāhu and the lower half the descending node (Ketu). He is the oppressor of the Sun and Moon, one or other of which, according to Puranic mythology, he swallows and thereby produces an eclipse. He is represented as a grotesque grinning monster with grisly hair and moustaches and two immense cannine teeth projecting from the upper jaw. In his right hand, he holds a crescent and in his left hand, a broken object which Stirling takes for a hatchet and Mitra for the sun, which really looks like a duplicate of the crescent held in the right hand. He has no legs. The ninth figure is that of Ketu or the descending node, the oppressor of the stars. The lower half of his body takes the form of a serpent's tail, which coils right and left in such a way that the loops at either side give the impression of a figure, seated cross-legged like the other figures.

In the central projections, of the three sides (south, west and north) there are, at this level, three very fine statues of the Sun-God, carved in full relief, on large chlorite slabs. The images can be approached by two flights of steps on the right and left, which also serve to separate the main temple from the smaller temples

---

[62] Archaeological Survey of India, *Annual Reports*, 1903-04.

on its three sides.

The statue on the south side is 8'6" high, has the matted hair of an ascetic and wears stockings, elaborate dhotī and ornaments. At the feet of the figure sits his legless charioteer Aruṇa, driving the seven horses. There are number of attendants carved on the pedestal and on the black slab, some seated and others standing. Near the shoulders of the deity is a small seated figure of Viṣṇu on the proper left, and of Brahmā on the right.

The image on the north side differs from the other two, in as much as the Sun-God is shown here as riding on a fine horse elaborately decorated with ornaments. The charioteer has been dispensed with, but in other details the statue is similar to the other two figures.

A fine statue of Sun-God measuring 6'3" x 3' was found in the interior, standing on a pedestal against one of the massive pillars. He is in the chariot of the seven horses, which is driven by his charioteer Aruṇa. His two hands are broken, but we can see two lotuses on his two sides near his face. He is well ornamented with necklace, Kuṇḍala, crown, etc. He has put on udarabandha and also a sacred thread. On his two sides, there are one male and one female figures. These figures are not clear. So we say that these are Daṇḍa and Piñgala or his two wives Śaṁjā and Nikṣubhā, as they are common in Sanskrit literature as well as in many of the existing images.

The uniqueness of this temple lies in the fact that the temple presents an obvious look of a Sun-temple, on account of its specific design of a Solar chariot

An illustration from *Chidambaram* Mūrtivijñāna[63] evidently represents Sūrya as composed of Brahmā, Maheśvara and Viṣṇu i.e. Trimūrti (so he has three heads), though the symbols held in the hands do not clearly indicate the same. He has six hands. In his two hands he is holding *lotus bud* and *a book.* Two hands are in the pose of *Abhaya and Varada Mudrā.* Out of the remaining

---

[63] See Sachau, *Alberuni's India*, and also Khare, G.H., *Murtivijnana*, fig. 60. p. 146.

two hands, one hand holds the *Śankha* and the other hand holds the discus. On both the sides, there are his two wives Rājñī and Nikṣubhā. The figure is in standing position. The figure is bare-footed. It is natural for South Indian sculpture. He is well ornamented. He has put on the udarabandha or a sacred thread. On the pedestal are shown seven horses, driven by Aruṇa, who, though believed to be without legs, is here represented with them. But within the flaming orb is recognised the God Nārāyaṇa (Viṣṇu)[64], whose body is golden, who assumes the forms of Brahmā in the morning, Maheśvara (Śiva) in the mid-day and Viṣṇu in the evening. In this composite form, he is on a lotus pedestal with crocodile ear-rings (Makara-Kuṇḍala) and a crown and exhibits in his hands the conch and discus and all the characteristic weapons of the Trimūrti.

An image of Sūrya in the *British Museum*[65] at London, bears on the base above the horses an inscription in very corrupt Sanskrit, in Nāgarī character of the 10th cent. AD.

Oṁ Indranīlamaṇī Śiṣyaḥ Śilāya Buddhiḥ sālinā/
Ghaṭitāya Kṛtajñena Amritena Suśilpinā.

"This image has been carved in stone by the wise, grateful and good artist Amrita, pupil of Indranīlamaṇi."

Here we have the names of two Gaudian sculptors, Amrita and his teacher Indranīlamaṇī. In order to determine, how far the claim of Amrita as a suśilpin, good artist is justified we should consider two halves of this image, the upper half and the lower half, separately. The upper half of the back slab is very tastefully decorated with the floral and animal motives usually found on later Pāla sculptures. The upper half of the image of Sūrya itself forms rather an integral part of this decorative scheme than an independent sculpture, though the beautifully modelled torso and

[64] In the Prayāgaratna the Sun is invoked alongwith the gods Agni and Rudra. The former is described as the presiding deity of the Sun-God while the latter is the chief source of his energy. See *South Indian Gods and Goddesses*, Chap. VII, p. 238.

[65] Chanda, *Medieval Indian Sculpture in the British Museum*, London, 1936, Chap. VI, pl. xx, pp. 66-67.

the arms throb with life; and with half-shut eyes the god is looking towards the earth below with complacency. In this part of the image, the artist follows convention with consummate skill. In the lower half, actuated by the aesthetic impulse, he breaks away from convention by ordering the subordinate figures, in such a manner as to leave sufficient plain background, to project them in the best possible way.

In this sculpture, Sūrya himself and all his attendants wear boots. To the extreme right and the extreme left of the group, two women (called Uṣā and Pratyuṣā) are moving threateningly with bow and arrow, behind the woman on the right stands the corpulent and pot-bellied Piñgala holding a pen in his right hand and an inkpot in his left hand. Next to him stands a female, a wife of the God, holding a chaurī. To the left of Sūrya stands another wife holding chaurī and the second male attendant Daṇḍa in tribhanga posture, offering protection with his right hand. Sūrya stands erect and his body is in a state of stiff repose, but his attendants are in alert pose. At the feet of Sūrya stands the Earth Goddess, and in front of her is his winged charioteer, Aruṇa guiding the horses with outspread wings. The seven horses carved in high relief on the base do not lack movement.

THE IMAGE OF SŪRYA — THE KHMER ART[66]

"68-Sūrya? (KP. 40, 1) — standing image. His head has one halo but without rays. Yet it is without doubt that its identification is with Sūrya, in his two hands, raised upto the shoulders, arc two lotuses (closed). This image at the first impression looks like the Egyptian.

69-Sūrya ? (KP. 40, 2) — very short image. The head-dress is cylindrical. The horses are missing, halo is full of rays. His hair is hanging on the shoulders. But the figure is without ornaments. His dress is very long reaching up to the knees. The girdle

---

[66] Louis Mallert, *Catalogue general des Collections,* Musée Blanchard de la Bross, Saigon, 1937, Ton.I, pp. 76-78.

is very tight. This torso is very good. The hands and legs are missing.

70-Sūrya (KP. 40, 3) — very short figure of Sūrya. It has neither hands nor legs. The head-dress is round. The head is surrounded by rays. He is dressed like an iron cuirass. Two broken figures are placed near the shoulders. It seems that the God must be holding two things up to the height of the chest, in the style of Sūrya (KP. 40. 1)."

A PART OF LEFT SIDE FRIEZE OF NINE PLANETS (THE ART OF KHMÉR)

A preserved fragment in good condition — where only two figures are there. On the left side, the figure of Sūrya is seated on a chariot drawn by two galloping horses. But its head is missing. On the right side, the figure is of *Soma*, seated on a pedestal. The images have put on the short coat with strips. There are ornaments on the ears and near the neck. The mukuṭa is conical. The image has moustache. The attributes are the lotuses. The group is against two recesses. It is fixed by an arc near the bracket (10th, 11th century)[67]

PANEL OF NINE PLANETS

On a beautiful pedestal, there are nine figures seated. Eight of these figures before the pedestal, are accompanied by animal figures in profile to identify the figures. It is known as their *vāhana*. The heads of all are missing. From the left to the right we can recognise Sūrya, the sun, on a chariot drawn by seven horses. His hands are up to the shoulders, the attributes which are without doubt the lotuses. The figure seems to have a chignon on the side.

One of the most important discoveries made in Burma, is that of a stone figure of Sūrya on a hill at Mrohaung[68] in the

---

[67] Louis Malleret, *Catalogue general des Collections*, Musée Blanchard de la Brosse, Saigon, 1937, Ton.I, p. 111.

[68] Archaeological Survey of India, *Annual Reports* (Burma Circle) 1922-23, pl. xxxiii, fig.c, p. 123.

Akyab district. The stone which measures 5'3" in height including the tenon beneath, depicts on the obverse face Sūrya riding in a chariot drawn by seven horses. It is much defaced but enough remains to show, that it wears a high head-dress and that it has only two hands both lifted up to the level of the shoulders with something indistinguishable held in them. The figure of the chariot driver is missing. It is flanked on either side by a small female figure, one appears to be holding a bow and the other an arrow. The reverse face is with an inscription in North Indian character, which has also weathered much and is practically illegible. But from what remains of it, can be made out that it is written in a variety of Gupta characters, belonging to about the 8th cent. AD and may be earlier. It is, only figure of its kind and the earliest one, that has been found either in Arakan or in Burma proper. Besides, with the stone sculptures of Hindu gods in Wuntitaung, a hillock in the neighbourhood of the above hill, it shows the strong Hindu influence in early times. The first mention of Mrohaung in the Arakanese chronicles refer to the 10th cent. AD.

At Khair Khaneh (Afghanistan), Hackin found out one very beautiful image of Sūrya which is of marble (Fig. 13). He has no halo. He is dressed like a Sassanian king and wearing a round apron-like tunic fringed with pearls seated on a chariot, having two horses and driven by a charioteer Aruṇa. There are two figures with him. These two figures near the God are Daṇḍa and Piñgala (according to the Matsya Purāṇa). This very ancient sculpture of Khair Khaneh (Vth cent.) shows, that, the Sun cult was very well-known, in the oriental countries. According to Hackin, two figures near the Sun-God, are not doubtful and the Sun-God with his assistants in India, is a foreign element. But, it seems that there must be four horses the way in which they are shown, they must be hidden by the two horses behind[69].

[69] See Hackin, J., *Researches Archaeologique au Col de Khair Khaneh Prés de Kabul*, 1936, Chap. III, fig. 5.

DESCRIPTIONS OF IMAGES (UNPUBLISHED)

Several images of sun are noted by scholars. They are not illustrated, so, only their descriptions are noted here.

The Mathura Museum[70] No. 1559 shows a panel of two Sūryas, wearing Iranian coats, trousers and buskin boots and holding sheathed swords and lotuses.

In Boston Museum[71], there is only one image of Sun-God Sūrya (No. 21.1706), squatting figure with knees raised (i.e. riding in a car), wearing a conical cap or helmet, chain armour, a Dhotī (?) and boots (?) or socks, also ear-rings, necklace, bracelets and perhaps a sacred thread. The right hand holding a club (Gadā), the left a staff (Daṇḍa). Horses are represented below to the right and the left, the front pair (of the four) only being clearly defined.

Whether or not the deity is intended to be represented as wearing high boots, as is usual in the early northern forms with Iranian affinities, cannot be clearly determined in the worn state of the sculpture. Apparently, some kind of leg armour is intended. The absence of any indication of toes, suggests the use of a sock or boot.

KAILASA[72]

In the back aisle of the cave, are a series of pretty large sculptures. At the east end is Viṣṇu as Sūrya or the Sun-God, with two hands, holding flowers and with female attendants on each side holding buds and male with spear and oval shield. In the same cave, another image of Sūrya[73] is described, but its photograph is not given. It is said that, it is one of the rare images ever found in India. It is on the south side of the entrance porch and partly on the west wall of the Gopuram of Kailāsa. Here is a

---

[70] Agarvala, V.S., *The Handbook of the Mathura Museum.*

[71] Coomaraswamy, A.K., *The Catalogue of the Indian Collections*, Museum of Fine Arts, Boston, Parts I & II, p. 46.

[72] Fergusson and Burgess, *The Caves and Temples of India,* p. 459.

[73] Burgess, J., *The Caves of Ellora and other Brahmanical and Jain Caves in Western India*, p. 37.

large sculpture of Śiva in the chariot of Sun, drawn by the four horses as Vedas, with Brahmā as his charioteer, armed with the bow (Himālaya) which he draws against an enemy. This sculpture is also found in the Daśāvatāra cave. In front of this sculpture, are several panels with the groups of small figures, which are of no use to describe here.

There is a Sun-image, in the India Museum at Calcutta[74], with the usual attributes and attendants. It is on the left of the stone image of Harihara. In a panel below, are depicted the seven horses of chariot and the figure of the charioteer Aruṇa, can also be recognised between the two legs of the central figure. The execution of this sculpture is quite crude, and shows a debased style which suggests a late date for it (perhaps 11th or 12th cent.). This is also supported by the staring look of the eyes. The introduction of the Buddha and Sūrya by the side of Harihara, constitutes the chief iconographic importance of this image.

A.K. Coomaraswamy[75] describes the image of the Sun-God in the Worcester Art Museum (Lucknow). Here, the Sun-God is not as an independent image, but it is in the slab of Navagraha i.e. the nine planets. He says, "This sand-stone slab with eight figures in high relief is an important example of Indian sculpture in the Worcester Art Museum. The composition belongs to a well-known type representing the nine planets (Navagraha), that is to say Planetary and other stellar deities corresponding to the Ādityas (Varuṇa, etc.) of Vedic mythology. Beginning from the left hand side the figures represent successively: Sūrya (The Sun), Candra (The Moon), Mangala (Mars), Budha (Mercury), Bṛhaspati (Jupiter), Śukra (Venus), Śani (Saturn) and Rāhu, the ascending node of the Moon, the ninth figure, representing Ketu, the descending node of the Moon, is now lacking, a small part of the slab on the right hand side being broken away. There is no inscription, nor the deities distinguished by any representation of their animal vehicle."

---

[74] Archaeological Survey of India, *Annual Reports*, 1930-34, p. 257.
[75] *Marga*, Vol.VI, No.3, 1953.

Sūrya, on the extreme left, is represented with a necklace, jewelled head-dress, a corslet of chain armour, loin cloth and girdle, loose shawl or sash falling below the knees, the hands are raised to the level of the shoulders, each hand holding a lotus (Padma). Of these elements the two lotuses are characteristic of Sūrya in a majority of his images, particularly those of later date and the chain armour is characteristic of the earlier 'northern' costume, whether the Worcester figure is to be understood as wearing boots or is barefooted like the six figures following, cannot be definitely determined. Coomaraswamay gives his opinion — "The Worcester group of the Navagraha may be assigned at least tentatively to the later part of the Gupta period (AD 320-650), in some sense the "best" i.e. the most fully evolved and yet still creative period of Indian Art. The forms are full and essentially sculpturesque; the art is still an art of volumes, and not yet one of boundaries, as it has become in the Lucknow Navagraha referred to above. Notwithstanding that six of the eight figures are iconographically identical, each is individually and sensitively treated. All are more graceful and have more movement than is usual in the preceding Kushan period. The Sūrya type is intermediate in character between early and late forms. The differentiation of the "low caste" Rāhu from the more aristocratic powers is very marked and exhibits admirably the great range of expressive power to be recognised in Gupta Art. It is upon such general grounds that the work is here assigned to the Gupta period. It is undoubtedly of North Central Indian origin and though not in the common red-stone so much used at Mathura, may be of that school."

SOME OF THE SCULPTURES IN THE MUSEUM OF THE BANGIYA SAHITYA PARISHAD[76]

(1) No. H(a) 1/378: A slab arched at the top and terminating in a Kīrtimukha flanked by two small floral devices in bold relief

[76] Ganguly, Manmohan, *Handbook to the Sculptures in the Museum of the Bangīya Sāhitya Parishad.*

containing the kilted figure of Sūrya standing erect in Samapāda sthānaka pose on a Padmapīṭha resting on a bhadrapīṭha of the navaratha type. The Kaṇṭha, or the verticle recess of the pedestal is carved with seven horses, some of which are damaged. The crown or the Kiriṭa of the Sun-God and the two forearms holding lotus-stalks are broken and the face mutilated. The image is carved in the round from the shoulder down to the foot. The god has a pointed nimbus behind, showing three lines of flames at the top and two lines at the bottom; he is richly bejewelled and wears elaborately carved Kaṇṭhahāra (necklace), Keyūra, Karṇakuṇḍala (ear-rings), Karnapūra, Śirobandha with the puritans and the Kāñchi set with the central gem (Madhyamaṇī). The breast-plate is visible, wavy locks of hair fall gracefully on the shoulder and in front of the breast, the small ringlets of hair are noticeable on the forehead just below the Śirobandha. Though mutilated, the pointed tilaka mark on the forehead is still visible. A small dagger passes through the girdle and is attached to the right of the image, on the left hangs a sword. The top of the boot is curled up. The god is flanked on either side by a kilted female figure standing on a Padmapīṭha in Samabhaṅga pose, one of the two figures bending in Kaṭihasta pose and the other holding something rectangular (perhaps a book). These are two of the four consorts of the Sun-God, e.g. Rājñī, Savarṇā, Suvarcasā and Chāyā. On the two extreme ends stand two kilted male figures, the one on the extreme left is kilted and bejewelled and stands with the right leg stepping forward, he holds the pen and ink-stand in the two hands, he is identified as Piñgala. On the right side stands Daṇḍa grasping the handle of a sword with the left hand. On either side of the main image and near the base of the Padmapīṭhas of the consorts of the god, stand two female figures in the pose of shooting arrows. These are Uṣā and Pratyuṣā. In front and on the padmapīṭha stands the figure Prithivī. The figure of Aruṇa, driving the chariot, is much mutilated. The makara terminals of the toraṇa behind are nicely carved, below these stands the Śārdula on either side with one foot resting on the back of a couchant elephant, over the terminals stand the Kinnara and

Kinnarī. The slab is flanked at the top by the flying figures of the Gandharvas carrying garlands.

(2) No. H(a) 2/429: The whole slab is arched and pointed. The whole slab from the foot to the crown represents the aureole, its edges simulating flames, it is surrounded by an umbrella at the apex, below it and on either side of the image is seen the flying Gandharva carrying a garland with his consort with folded hands. The image stands in a Samapāda sthānaka pose, on a full-blown lotus (Padmapīṭha) resting on a low pedestal, carved on its face with the figures of seven horses. It has a torque or a neck-lace interlaced on both sides of the breast. It is kilted, beaded tassels hang from the waist band, it has on its person bracelets (Valaya), elaborate armlet, Kuṇḍala (ear-ring) and a richly carved Kiriṭa mukuṭa with the Śirobandha. Both the right and left hands of the figure, hold lotus-stalks and are in the pose of granting protection or Abhaya, but the thumb touches the ring finger and forms a circle on the palm. The hands are in the tripatākā hasta pose. The lotuses on the both sides of the image are supported by something (?). It has a small female figure (Goddess Earth or Prithivī) standing on the lotus in front. The image is flanked on the left by a bearded, squat and dwarfish figure (Piñgala) wearing a plain Kiriṭamukuṭa with a fillet. It is flanked on the right by a standing figure (Daṇḍa) in the tribhanga form holding a sword in the right hand, the left touching the waist (Kaṭī hasta pose). At the foot of the main central image, is seen the standing figure of a female, with a lotus on either side with the right upraised hand in the Abhayamudrā, and the left hand in the pose of conferring a boon, below it, is a seated figure of Aruṇa with whip in the right hand and holding a duck (?) in the left hand, the bird resting on the back of the horse, in the middle of the group. The portion projecting from the pedestal in the centre, is carved with a female figure on either side, in the pose of shooting an arrow. It is carved in the centre with the figures of three devotees.

(3) No. H(a) 3/232: A fragment arched at the top from the

upper part of an image of Sūrya surrounded by eleven Ādityas of whom only six exist. The peculiar form of hair, hanging in two tiers behind the shoulder of the image, is noteworthy, the face is as usual but injured, the conventional *trivali* marks on the neck are visible. The breast plate of the main figure and the lotus held in the right hand are noticeable. The Ādityas, according to the Viśvakarmaśāstra, are four handed, whereas they are two-handed in the present case, and hold the same attribute of the Padma or lotus in their hands.

(4) No. H(a) 4/267: The upper part of an image of Sūrya standing inside a panel surmounted by a beaded trefoil arch having at its top the Kīrtimukha representation and flanked on either side by a flying figure carrying a garland. Sūrya wears a Kiriṭamukuṭa, Tāṭanka or ear-ring, armlet, bracelet, elaborate necklace and holds two full-blown lotuses in his two hands. The left hand of the image is in tripatākā pose, on the two sides of pilasters are carved the seated figures in two tiers, probably the Ādityas, two such figures only exist. The pupils of the eye of the main image are shown.

(5) No. H(a) 6/249: A pedestal of the image of Sūrya showing his horses, the one in the centre being broken. It is of the Pañcaratha type, the fillet at the top being carved with the petals of lotus. The feet of the god resting on a flat lotus and his attendant figures are noticeable. The fragment of Uṣā on the left side about to dart an arrow is also seen. The horses are saddled, the reins are nicely carved. The pedestal is carved with the figures of two devotees, one male and the other a female.

In this museum, there is one slab of Navagraha. Among the Navagrahas there is first the image of Surya and then the images of other grahas. Here Sūrya is described as seated on lotus and wearing a truncated Kiriṭa, two full-blown lotuses are noticed behind his shoulders, the stalks being held in the two hands, the right hand is mutilated. Then Soma and other planets are shown."

Sculptures of medieval India in the British Museum at London are described by Chanda[77] as —

[77] Chanda, *Medieval Indian Sculptures in the British Museum*, London, 1936.

"Among the post-Gupta sculptures we find the description of the Sun-image as follows:

(1) (No. 84, 40" × 15") Sūrya is two-armed and holds two lotus flowers in his two hands. He has one wheeled chariot driven by seven horses carved on the base. On two sides of the Sun-God, on the base are his two wives, Savarṇā and Chāyā, holding chauris and his two attendants[78], Piñgala to the right holding pen and inkpot, and Daṇḍa to the left. The female figure between the feet of Sūrya is the Earth Goddess".

In the Gaudian or Pāla sculptures, there are two images of the Sun-Gods. They are described as follows:

(2) (No.58, 30" × 16") The Sun-god of the Gaudian School, is with a black slab rounded at the top and decorated only by scroll-work on the border. It is earlier in date (Early Pāla period). Another mark of early date of this image is the octagonal crown with flat top. The face of Sūrya is lifeless and blank. The god wears a breast-plate. One other uncommon feature of this image is that in the chariot there are two wheels, instead of one carved on the base. According to the Purāṇas Sūrya drives in a chariot having only one wheel and drawn by seven horses.

(3) (No. 57) Sūrya[79]: Here two male attendants with sword and shield and the representation of the reins of the horses held by the charioteer Aruṇa — traits that characterize the images of Sūrya belonging to the great temple Konaraka[80] indicates the Orissan origin of this image. The points of difference between this image and the images of Sūrya at Konaraka are no less striking. The swordsmen attending this image do not wear crowns on their heads, as the swordsmen attending the Konaraka images do. The figures of Daṇḍa and Piñgala and the two female Chauri bearers (wives), are carved on the Konaraka images (Piñgala with pen and inkpot on the left of Sūrya and Daṇḍa with staff on the right), but not on this image. It may, therefore, be inferred

---

[78] Compare Hemadri, p. 148.

[79] Chanda, *Medieval Indian Sculptures in the British Museum,* London , p. 71.

[80] Banerjee, R.D., *History of Orissa,* Vol.II, plates facing pp. 88 and 384.

that this image of Sūrya does not come from Konaraka, and is probably of an earlier date. The face of this Sūrya is expressionless, but the faces of the Konaraka images show absorption in meditation. The modelling of the main figure is stiff but the minor figures, the Vidyādharas, the two women holding bows and the horses on the base are full of movement.

"The five[81] seated images of the Grahas (planets) are undoubtedly from Konaraka, and probably belonged to the great temple of Sūrya. The pentafoiled arch and other features are also found in other known groups of images of the nine grahas from Konaraka. Only one of these figures, that of the seated Sūrya holding lotus flowers, can be identified. Other figures do not hold the attributes peculiar to the different grahas, but all hold garlands of beads in the right hand and a pot, probably containing nectar, in the left hand. A pot-bellied figure wearing a beard can be identified as Bṛhaspati (Jupiter). All these figures sit cross-legged and their eyes are half-shut but blank".

In supplementary catalogue of the Archaeological Collection of the *Indian Museum,* Calcutta, Bloch describes some of the Brahmanic sculptures. No. 3927 — "A sculpture of Sūrya, standing in his single wheeled chariot drawn by seven horses. The horses and the wheels are represented in the lowest part of the sculpture, Sūrya is represented with two hands holding two lotuses, both hands are broken. A sword hangs from the belt. In front of Sūrya is Aruṇa, seated, represented as driving the chariot. In his left hand, he holds the reins and in his right hand a stick. To the right of Sūrya, is an erect male figure holding in his right hand a pen and in his left hand an ink-pot, to the left, another male figure with a big staff in his hand. These two figures are probably representations of two planets. Over them, are two female figures in "Pratyālīḍha" and "Ālīḍha" postures represented as shooting arrows, they are probably the representations of Sun's rays. The figure of the Sun, as well as the other two

[81] Only three are at present exhibited in the British Museum, London (Nos. 100-104) by Chanda.

male figures are represented as wearing boots."

BIHAR

No. 3933 — A similar, but, a larger figure of Sūrya standing on a full-blown lotus, the horses and the charioteer are wanting. The two female figures with bows and arrows are standing, each on one side of the two male attendants.

No. 3928 — Similar sculpture. The female figures shooting arrows are in the "Āliḍha" and "Pratyāliḍha" postures and have been placed in front of the attending male figures. There are two figures of Vidyādharas, represented in the upper part of the slab, carrying garlands.

No. 5820 — A finely carved sculpture representing Sūrya in his chariot drawn by seven horses. In front, Aruṇa is seated and driving the horses. Between Aruṇa and Sūrya is a female figure, probably of Ushas or Dawn. The female figures shooting arrows are placed on the two sides of Aruṇa, to the right of Sūrya stands male figure, bearded and pot-bellied, holding in his hands an ink-pot and pen. By his side is a female figure with a chaurī in the right hand. To the left of Sūrya is a female figure with a chaurī in her right hand and by her side a male figure with a tapering crown. The right hand is on the breast of the figure and the left hand holds a sword. The sides of the slab are elaborately sculptured with figures of lions and elephants. The upper part of the slab shows two Vidyādharas with garlands. The two female attendants of Sūrya in this sculpture, as well as in other similar ones, are, his two wives – Samjñā and Chāyā.

No. 3925 — Sculpture represents the Sun in his single-wheeled chariot drawn by seven horses. Seven miniature horses and a wheel along the base, represent the car with horses. In front of Sūrya is Aruṇa represented, in the act of driving the chariot, to the right, a bearded male figure and at his side a female with bow and arrow. To the left a male figure holding something like a trident, and at his side another female figure with bow and arrow. The lower portions of the legs of the figures are covered by the chariot and are not visible.[82]

No. (without number) — A figure of Sūrya in his chariot, drawn by seven horses. Aruṇa is represented as driving the chariot. Upper part of a statue, including left arm, broken and lost. To the right, a male figure with a long staff and to the left a male figure with pen and ink-pot. The lower parts of legs do not appear and Sūrya carries his sword on his right side instead of the left.

No. 3934 — An erect figure of Sūrya. To the right the male figure with pen and ink-pot and to the left the figure with a long staff, probably the planet Mars (Maṅgala).

No.3930 — A statue of Sūrya in his chariot. In the front are represented seven horses, driven by Aruṇa. To the right of the figure of Sūrya the same male figure as above and to his right the female figure, represented as shooting arrows. To the left, another male figure with a sword (?) in his left hand and at his side another female figure, represented as shooting arrows. Portion of the slab, at the back of the statue is lost. In the upper part of the slab are figures of Vidyādharas with garlands.

No. 3929 — A figure of Sūrya in his chariot of seven horses driven by Aruṇa. To the right, the male figure with pen and ink-pot, and to the left, the male figure with a big staff, probably the Maṅgala graha or planet Mars.

No. 3926 — Two pieces of a broken sculpture representing Sūrya. The head of the figure and whole of its right hand are lost. To the right, a bearded figure, broken in the middle, and at his side a female figure, shooting arrows. To the left another male

[82] "It was a common Indian belief, often referred to in the Purāṇas, that Sūrya had no legs and arms. The burning heat emanating from his body had reduced him to an unsightly lump of flesh. This idea goes back to the oldest representations of Sūrya under the symbol of a wheel or a lotus, with nothing but a human face added to it. The famous image of Jagannath in Puri, has still preserved to us this ancient type of Sūrya; for Jagannath was originally a local form of the Sun-God, worshipped along the coast of the Eastern Sea. He was first associated with the cult of the Śaivas and only about five centuries ago with the cult of the Vaiṣṇavas." Bloch, *Supplementary Catalogue of the Archaeological Collection of the Indian Museum*, 1911 (Cabinet 20).

figure with a female figure shooting arrows.

No. 3924 — A similar sculpture, in a state of perfect preservation. In front, Aruṇa is driving the horses. At his back stands Uṣas, the Goddess of Dawn. To the right, the same bearded male figures as above and to the left, a male figure with a trident in his left hand, probably *Śanaiścara,* the planet Saturn. Two female figures shooting arrows are placed near the feet of the male figures. In the upper part of the slab, are two figures of Vidyādharas with garlands.

No. 4167 — A slab containing representations of the Navagrahas or nine planets. These are Ravi or the Sun, Soma or the Moon, Maṅgala or Mars, Budha or Mercury, Bṛhaspati or Jupiter, Śukra or Venus, Śanaiścara or Saturn, Rāhu and Ketu.[83]

No. 4168 — Another slab showing the nine planets (Grahas) standing inside small temples. A separate shrine has been assigned to each Graha.

No. 4169 — Another Navagraha slab in three pieces.

No. 3937 — Another numberless stone, in centre of the cabinet, with symbolical representation of Sūrya. The lotus is on the top of them, one of the old symbols, by which the Sun used to be represented in Ancient India".

In *South Indian Images of Gods and Goddesses* (p. 235) Shastri mentions that of the miscellaneous gods found in South Indian temples, mention may be made of the Navagrahas or "the nine planets", headed by the Sun.

"They are installed within the enclosed verandah round the central shrine of a temple with or without a special structure erected over them. The Sun stands in the centre and the others are fixed round him, each in a specific direction. The planets are highly respected and scrupulously worshipped by the people, as they are believed to influence the destinies of human beings... In

---

[83] Similar slabs are seen over the door of almost every temple in North India. It was a common belief of the Indians that the nine planets give stability to any building; hence the ceremony called Grahaśānti or expiation of the planets, which according to Yājñavalkya and others was to be performed before a house was built — J. Bloch.

the south, there does not appear to be any such class exclusively devoted to the Sun. The worship is common to all. Āditya-grahas (Sun-shrines) are mentioned in inscriptions of the eighth or ninth centuries of the Christian era, in the northern districts of the Presidency, in later times temples of Traipuruṣadeva are found dedicated to Sun, Śiva and Viṣṇu, with much prominence given to the first as indicated by the sculptures. Evidence of the building of separate Sun-temples in South India, earlier than the 12th cent. AD, has not yet been found. The only temple so far known to be dedicated to the Sun and his attendant planets exclusively, is the one at Sūriyanārkoyil[84] in the Tanjore District. "The central shrine of this temple, which faces the west, is dedicated to Sūrya, the Sun-God; near the image of the Sun-God are also placed those of Viśveśvara and his consort Viśālākṣī. The figure of Bṛhaspati is set up in front of the central and those of the other Grahas in small shrines constructed round the central shrine."[85]

SUN IMAGES IN THE SUN TEMPLES OF GUJARAT

Somanath and other mediaeval temples in Kathiawāḍa[86]. Sūtrapāḍā — The old shrine at Sūtrapāḍā (8 miles from Somanātha Pātaṇa) is between the village and the sea-shore, in a clump of trees in the fields and is dedicated to Sūrya. The present image of Sūrya, in this temple, is a late one; an inscription on the doorway stating that it was set up in Saṁvat 1357 (AD 1301) by one Thakur Vīsala Deva or Vājal Deva as written in the inscription.

Besides the temple, on its south side is a modern one of the Navagraha, or nine planets, but it is of little interest.

Thān[87] — At Thān which is on the railway, half way between Waḍhwāṇa and Rajkot, are a few objects of interest, among them being a temple of Sūrya which is of some note in the province. Thān is one of the most ancient places in India and the whole

[84] *Madras Epigraphical Report for 1908,* Part II, para 60.
[85] Rao, Gopinatha, *Elements of Hindu Iconography,* Vol.II, p. 323.
[86] Cousens, Archaeological Survey of India, *Imperial Series,* Vol.XIV, p. 41.
[87] Ibid., pl. XLVI-L, p. 46.

neighbourhood is holy ground. Thān, derives its name from the Sanskrit word *sthān* 'a place' as though it was the place haloed above all others by the residence of devout sages, but the excellence of its city and by its propinquity to famous shrines, such as that of Trinetreśvara now called Tarṇetara, the famous temple of the Sun at Kaṇḍolā and those of the snake-brethren Wāsuki and Bāṇḍuka, now known as Wāsaṅgī and Bāṇḍia Beli respectively.

One of the chapters of the Skanda Purāṇa is devoted to Trinetreśvara and the neighbourhood. This chapter is called Thān Purāṇa. Here we learn that "the first temple to the Sun was built by Rājā Māndhātā in the Satyayuga.... The central fortress was called Kaṇḍolā, and here was the celebrated temple of the Sun. Thān was visited also by Kṛṣṇa and his consort Lakṣmī... Now, according to modern tradition, the story is that Wāloji risked a battle, and Jām Abrā (or Abdā) was defeated and forced to return to Kachha.[88] Wāloji and his Kāṭhis now established themselves at Thān, and Wāloji in gratitude to the Sun, repaired the temple of that luminary on the Kaṇḍolā hill. This temple, as stated before, is said to have been founded by Rājā Māndhātā in the Satyayuga and there is no doubt that it is really a most ancient temple. It was, it is said, repaired by the celebrated Lākhā Phulāṇi. This temple has undergone so many repairs and rebuildings that the original structure has entirely disappeared, and its present appearance is by no means imposing. Then Sujāt Khān, in AD 1690, destroyed the temple of the Sun. In this battle, some say that "The Sun appeared in Wāloji's ranks in mortal form, riding on a white horse and that wherever this strange warrior went the enemy's men fell as though mow down with a sickle. After this the Kāṭhis devoted themselves more than ever to Sun worship".

There are the remnants of a still older shrine, which possibly stood where the present Sūrya temple stands, or they may have been brought from two ruined temples, which stood about a hundred and fifty yards to the south-east of the present temple, a

[88] *Indian Antiquary*, IV, p. 322.

portion of the basement and other remains of which still lie there. There is no definite indication, however, that temple was dedicated to Sūrya, except for an isolated image of Sūrya of doubtful age, built into the back wall of the courtyard.

The temple, as is the case with all those dedicated to Sūrya, faces the east or rising Sun, and within its shrine, is a modern image of that deity dressed in coloured clothes. The pillars in the hall of the temple are very plain and more or less clumsy in appearance, and there is no carving about the doorway of the shrine, as found in older temples.

The principal figure upon the back wall on the outside, as well as on the north and south sides, is that of Sūrya. He stands in the usual stereotyped pose, straight to the front, holding a full-blown lotus, by its long stalk, in each hand. Sūrya, alone of the gods has but two hands and he, alone, wears long boots almost up to the knees, of a distinctly Persian pattern, though he is very rarely found barefooted. Besides him, are his two wives, one on either side and not standing much higher than his knees. In all Hindu temple sculptures, subsidiary figures, in a group are made smaller than the principal one, the hero upon a memorial stone, for instance, will be shown of colossal size among a crowd of pigmies. Sūrya's seven horses, that draw his chariot, are here conspicuous by their absence. The door-frame, inserted in the outer wall round the temple, was very likely that of the hall of a temple that preceded the 1432 temple, the style being of an earlier period. An interesting feature upon it, is the representation, along the top, of the Navagrahas or nine planets, frequently seen upon mediaeval doorways in Rajputana and Central India. This particular example is not a very good one, the images being in one monotonous line, and, except for the big head, all alike. Cousens gives a representation of one, from Chitor in Rajputana, which is an older and better one. In the Thān one it will be seen that they are made up of the five planets proper, from left to right and the descending and ascending nodes. They are in this order, Sūrya or Ravi or the Sun, Candra or Soma or the moon, Maṅgala or Bhauma or Mars, Budha or Mercury, Bṛhaspati or Jupiter, Śukra or Venus, Śani or Saturn, Ketu the descending node and Rāhu the ascending node. Sūrya has his lotuses in his hands and behind the head of the Moon is the Crescent, while the next five have no particular distinguishing feature. Ketu is always shown as a large head without a body. Rāhu here, is much like the others, but he is more correctly depicted in the Chitor sculpture as a nāga figure with a serpent's tail. Beneath them, on the Thān doorway, is Gaṇapatī, upon the dedicatory block. In the middle, on the Chitor illustration, is Śiva, at the end to his right, is the three-headed Brahmā and at the other end is Viṣṇu.

Now Cousens, in the same work (pp. 9-10), concludes that "among the images of Hindu deities that of Sūrya, or the Sun-God, is frequently found, which as an exotic, was brought into India with Sun-Worship from Central Asia. It has been added to the Hindu Pantheon and occurs in temples dedicated to that deity, but sparsely upon others. On the fine old Sun-Temple at Moḍherā, but a few miles out of Kathiawada in the north, his image occurs scores of times, occupying all the important positions, including the dedicatory block above the hall doorway. The shrine had been blown up and destroyed but his seat, with his seven horses, was found buried in the débris. He is the only god represented as wearing boots which are of the Persian pattern, reaching almost to the knees, with slightly turned up toes and apparently made of soft pliable leather. He is also the only deity with two arms. In Wilkin's *Hindu Mythology*, the writer says that "Sūrya in the Puranic age, is described as having four arms but this evidently does not refer to this Persian importation, for among the hundreds of images in all parts of the country, that I have seen, I have never come across one with more than two. Very rarely, indeed, he is found barefooted. I know of only two examples; one illustrated in Bendall's *Journal of Literary and Archaeological Research in Nepal and North India* and one at an old Chalukyan temple in the Dharwar district. He is generally represented standing, holding in each hand, by its stalk, a full-blown lotus in the conventional form of a rosette. Usually a female figure stands upon either side of him, supposed to be his wives Saṁjñā and Chāyā. In their place, in the Nepal image, two male figures attend him, one holding a sword and the other a fly brush (Chowarī). In Rajputana he, frequently, has a long two-edged straight sword placed horizontally across behind the middle of his back, but this features, I have not seen elsewhere, nor do I know its meaning. Beneath him, are often shown the seven horses of his chariot, prancing forward, with Aruṇa (the Dawn) driving. A very spirited representation is found upon the wall in the courtyard of the great monolithic temple of Kailāsa at the Ellora Caves. The building of a temple to the sun, as early as AD 437–38, at Daśapura (Mandsor), is recorded in an inscription at that place, which suffering from neglect was repaired in AD 473–74, curiously, the name Khurāsan, whence Sun-worship appears to have come, is found in the name of two villages (Khurāsa) in the vicinity of Jūnagaḍha, at one of which a Sun-temple existed."

FIVE

COMPARISONS AND CONCLUSIONS

We may now proceed to consider individually the several features of an image of the Sun-God.

THE BOOTS OF THE SUN-GOD

The Matsya Purāṇa after recounting how the feet of the Sun-God were left unfinished by Viśva-Karmā adds (p. 31, Vanga Vashi edition), "So in the matter of the worship of the Sun, no one anywhere fashions his feet. If it is done, it gives leprosy. In picture, as well as in images placed in temples, the devotee should carefully refrain from conceiving the feet of the Sun-God." The Bṛhatsaṁhitā also directs that the body of the Sun-God should be hidden upto the thighs or the breast.[1]

In the earliest images, the God is made to stand in such a manner in the hollow of the car that his legs are invisible, as is the case with the image of the Sun-God on the Bodhagaya railing[2], as well as with the image at Ellora.[3] The images of the Sun-God from Bihar, now in the Indian Museum[4], similarly do not figure the legs of the God. In the Bengal images, another expedient was employed. The sculptors fashioned out the outlines of the legs of the God, but like the Divine Artificer of old, left them uncarved. The uncarved portion thus appeared, as if covered by leggings or boots, but they were not so in reality. Thus, the so-called boots of the Sun-God, are probably nothing but the rough outlines of Sūrya's uncarved legs.

---

[1] The words Uru (thigh) and Uraḥ (breast) being very much alike, led earlier to a confusion of meaning as is evident from some images which are represented only with the head and part of the breast while others are represented down to the thighs.

[2] Raja Rajendra Lal Mitra's *Bodhagaya* or Cunningham's *Archaeological Survey Report,* Vol.VI.

[3] Rao, Gopinatha, *Elements of Hindu Iconography*, pl. LXXXVIII, fig.2.

[4] *Supplementary Catalogue,* p. 78, No. 3925 and the next one on the next page.

The following points, however, are in favour of their being taken as boots or leggings:

1. The top of this uncarved portion is sometimes found ornamented and pointed outwards like a dog's tongue, while the toe is sometimes fashioned like the toes of shoes used in Upper India, which in turn probably owe their turned-up form of toe to use in mountainous countries.
2. The two wives of the Sun-God and his two male attendants also have their legs and feet similarly carved. There may be some reason in leaving the legs of the Sun-God uncarved, but there is absolutely no reason why his attendants should be similarly treated. The Bṛhatsaṁhitā directs that the Sun-God should be given a "northern dress" (Udīcya Vesha") while the passage of the Matsya Purāṇa quoted by Rao[5] directs that "his attendants, Daṇḍa and Piñgala, also should be dressed in northern fashion also. The sculptors may have taken advantage of this general direction for "northern fashion" to give the Sun-God, as well as his attendants, boots and thus evade representing the Sun's legs. It should be mentioned, however, that I have not succeeded in finding any text in which the legs of the Sun-God are expressly directed to be covered by long boots or leggings."

THE ORNAMENTS AND APPAREL OF THE SUN-GOD

The most notable among them are his girdle, his breast-plate or armour and his double cloth ("Vastra-yugma samopetam"). The first two are practically universal, but the double cloth, though present in most of the Bengal images of the Sun-God, are occasionally absent. The girdle always takes the form of a highly ornamental belt, furnished with a dagger on each side, perhaps an accompaniment of the northern dress. The breast-plate most often takes the form of a knot formed on the chest by the interlacing of lines passing round the shoulders and under the arms,

[5] Rao, Gopinatha, *Elements of Hindu Iconography.*

but sometimes it takes the form of a thin ornamental chuddar, crossed over the chest, and of such fine texture that the body shows through it.

Of the pair of cloths required to be given to the Sun-God, one is that which the God wears as a dhotī and which is held fast round the waist by the girdle. The second one is sometimes folded and hung in front from the girdle and sometimes rolled like a chuddar and attached to some portion of the body.

The other ornaments of Sūrya, viz. the necklace, the ear-ring, the crown, etc. do not call for special mention, though, as has been suggested to me, they may ultimately prove of importance, when discussing the original provenance of the Sun-God.

THE WIVES AND CHILDREN OF THE SUN-GOD

Sūrya, as we have already seen, had originally two wives, Uṣā and Saraṇyu, who became Sureṇu in the Bhaviṣya Purāṇa. The earthly double (Mahīmayī chāyā) of Sureṇu, who was called either Chāyā or Nikṣubhā, was added later on as the third wife of Sūrya.

In the Bhaviṣya Purāṇa (79-9), the etymology of the name Nikṣubhā is given, and it appears that the word is formed from the root *su*-to bring forth. Nikṣubhā is explained there as an appellation of the earth, because she creates the mortals, the disembodied spirits and the gods, and supports them with food as sweets, as nectar, herbs[6] and wines. The term "earthly double" is significant, and when we find that Dyau (the Firmament) is mentioned as one of the alternative names of Sureṇu, daughter of Viśwakarmā or Tvaṣṭṛ, we at once see that the Vedic pair Dyāvā-Pṛthivī (The Earth and the Firmament) were conceived as the two wives of the Sun-God, an extremely natural conception.

The intermediate stage in the growth of this idea may be found in the 4th part of the 15th chapter of the Aitareya Brāhmaṇa[7], where the Goddess Dyau, Uṣas, Go and Pṛthivī are

[6] *Nikṣubhā Sūrate Yasmādannauṣadhi Surāmṛtaiḥ/*
Martyān Pitṛnśca devānśca tenabhūrnikṣubhā smṛtāḥ//

[7] Bangiya Sahitya Parishat edition, edited by Trivedi, p. 321.

said to be "coupled" with (i.e. married to) Sūrya by the previous invocation of Sūrya, before they themselves are invoked.

The principal wives of the Sun-God are, therefore, three in number, Uṣas, Dyau and Pṛthivī i.e. the Dawn, the Firmament and the Earth. Uṣas stands by herself, and only rarely has Sandhyā (the evening) added to her as the co-wife of the Sun-God. Dyau has several names as Rājñī, Saṁjñā, Dyau, Twaṣṭṛ, Prabhā, Suvarchasā, etc. who are sometimes differentiated as individual personalities. The third one is variously called Nikṣubhā, Chāyā or Pṛthivī. It is curious that Uṣas, who is so important a goddess in the Rigveda, is hardly mentioned as a wife of Sūrya in the Purāṇas or Śilpa-śāstras, probably because she had no children. While the later two are always prominently mentioned. The Bengal sculptors, however, hardly ever failed to represent the miniature figure of Uṣas in front of the Sun-God, between the God himself and his charioteer, Aruṇa — it is exactly the place assigned to her in the Rigveda.

The following appear to be the main children of Sūrya — from Uṣas — none. She is said always to retain her youth. From Sureṇu — Vaivasvata, Manu, Yama and a daughter Yamī or Yamunā. From Nikṣubhā — Śani, Sāvarṇī, Manu and a daughter Tapati. From Sureṇu — in her form of a mare — the twin Aświns and Revanta.

THE CHARIOT OF THE SUN-GOD

The Matsya Purāṇa (Ad. 125), from verses 38 to the end is devoted to the description of the one-wheeled car of the Sun. The description is extremely interesting, as it is clear from the beginning that not a material car but an allegorical one is being described. Unfortunately, the passage is rather obscure, and is difficult to understand, without a knowledge of Indian Astronomy.

The Chariot of the Sun moves on a single wheel (the apparent unceasing motion of the Sun from north to south and south to north?), but it has also eight smaller wheels (the orbits of the planets?). The length of the pole is twice the middle part. (Does it mean to suggest that the path is elliptical ?). The different parts of the chariot are composed of different measures of time, ranging from seconds to aeons. The chariot of the Sun, has got some sort of connection with the pole star, but I cannot follow what is exactly meant. It appears that the chariot is said to be attached to the Pole Star by strings, round which it is said to be revolving like a potter's wheel.

The charioteer of the Sun is Aruṇa, the elder brother of Garuḍa, the famous bird of Viṣṇu. The story of the premature birth of Aruṇa is to be found in the Mahābhārata and need not be repeated here. He was only half formed on account of his premature birth and is represented as such on images of the Sun-God. Aruṇa, literally means the first ruddy gleam of the coming Dawn which he undoubtedly personifies, and as such is correctly placed in front of an image of the Sun-God. Behind Aruṇa is placed Dawn (Uṣas), and the Sun-God is placed immediately behind the Dawn.

THE SEVEN HORSES OF THE SUN-GOD

Macdonell (Vedic Mythology, p. 31) says that Sūrya's horses represent his rays, which are seven in number.[8] The later Purāṇas, while enumerating the seven rays of the Sun, are, however, unanimous in stating that the seven horses are the Seven Metres — Gāyatri, Bṛahatī, Uṣṇik, Jagatī, Pankati, Anuṣṭubha and Triṣṭubha.[9]

The seven rays, as Macdonell states, are already mentioned in the Vedas. Kūrmapurāṇam[10] says that the Sun has innumerable rays, of which seven are the chief. These are Susumṇā, Harīkesha, Viśwakarmā, Viśwaśraba, Sanjadvasu, Arbhavasu and Swaraka. They are evidently of different colours, as each is said to nourish a different planet and each planet is given a different hue in the Hindu astronomy. It appears, that the spectrum

---

[8] Reference is given to the 16th Rik of the 61st Sūkta of the 8th Maṇḍala of Ṛgveda, but the reference seems to be wrong as that Rik speaks of Rudra and not of Sūrya or his rays.

[9] Viṣṇudharmottara, Khaṇḍa III (Ad. 67, verses 11-12).

[10] Kūrmapurāṇam – Bangabhashi edition, pp. 186, 188.

was well known in India.

The first ray Suṣumṇā nourishes the Moon and it is said to shine slantingly upwards. The rest nourish the planets Mercury, Venus, Mars, Jupiter and Saturn respectively.

THE ATTENDANTS OF THE SUN-GOD

The three wives of the Sun-God, who invariably accompany him, have already been enumerated. On the left stands the daughter of Viśvakarmā, and on the right her duplicate, who belongs to the Earth; and immediately in front of the Sun-God stands Dawn. His charioteer, Aruṇa also has already been noticed.

The other attendants are the two male ones on the two sides, and two miniature female ones at the two extremities. Of the former, the one to the right is always represented with pen and ink-stand in his hands. The left one mostly has a sword in his right hand, sometimes a staff, rarely a conch-shell.

All the authorities are practically unanimous in calling the figure on the left as Daṇḍa, Daṇḍi or Daṇḍanāyaka, meaning Skanda, the leader of the heavenly hosts. But in some images the image of Skanda is separately represented elsewhere and so he may have also been taken by some as Yama, one of the sons of the Sun-God.

The figure on the right is usually called Piñgala. He is represented as a bearded, pot-bellied man with pen and inkstand in his hands. He is usually taken as the God-Agni (Fire)[11] as he resembles that god in having a beard.

In Bhaviṣya Purāṇa (Chap. 124) he is expressly called Agni, engaged in recording the good and evil deeds of people and called Piñgala, because of his Piñgala or tawny colour.

But, he was also sometimes taken as the God Vidhātā (the disposer), i.e. Brahmā, is apparent from (Chap. 261, p. 902) of

[11] "Agni should be given the sacred thread and he should have long beards. He should have a water pot in his left hand and rosary in his right". Matsya Purāṇa (p. 903) – Bangabhashi Edition.

Matsya Purāṇa (Bangabhasi edition), where Vidhātā with pen and ink-stand in his hands, is directed to be placed on one side of Sūrya. This is further corroborated by the statement found in the Bhaviṣya Purāṇa itself (Chap. 140), that the Maga Brahmins, the worshippers of Sūrya, used to wear beards, because Brahmā on the chariot of the Sun-God, and the Sun-God himself, used to wear beards.

THE FOREIGN INFLUENCE

From the description of the image of the Sun-God, two important points of historical significance, are to be noted; the dress of Sūrya and those of Daṇḍa and Piñgala are of Udīcya type. His girdle is called Aviyānga or Viyānga. We find similar references to the image of the Sun-God in the Bhaviṣya Purāṇa, the Viṣṇudharmottara Purāṇa and the Bṛhatsaṁhitā of Varāha Mihira. As R. G. Bhandarkar says, this was the same as the Aivyāonghen of the Avesta language, which signifies the Kusti worn by the Parsees at present.[12]

About this foreign influence, the image and in the worship of the Sun, it will be worthwhile to quote the opinion of R.G. Bhandarkar from his *Vaiṣṇavism and Śaivism* — "The Sun was a God, worshipped in early times, and his cult did not disappear as his orb was daily visible. But, he became the object of sectarian worship, sometime later. By the 3rd cent. of the Christian Era, another cult of the sun was introduced from Persia. It took root in the Indian soil and prevailed for a long time in North-Western India, a good many splendid temples having been erected from time to time for his worship. A special caste of priests of the name of Magas was associated with the cult, and the masses of the Hindu population adopted it as if it had been indigenous to the country".

According to R.G. Bhandarkar the images of the Sun that are

---

[12] For further discussion see *Vaiṣṇavism and Śaivism*, pp. 153-155 and 157, Article 160 and also see Rao, Gopinatha, *Elements of Hindu Iconography*, Vol.1, pt. II, pp. 301-06.

found in the extant remains of the temples of Sūrya from Multan, down to Cutch have boots reaching upto the knees and a girdle round the waist and with one hanging downwards.

As V. S. Agarvala says in his work, *Gupta Art,*[13] Sūrya images of ancient Indian type with a chariot of four horses are known in the early art of Bodhagaya, Bhājā and Anantaguphā. A new form of Sūrya clad in northern dress (Udīcyaveśa) and wearing long boots became the usual feature in Kuṣāna images, influenced by the Magian Sun-worship from Persia. The Persian influence is even more strongly marked in the Gupta images not only of the Sun-God, but also of his two attendants Daṇḍa and Piñgala, the latter a pot-bellied figure holding a pen and inkpot.

At Khair Khaneh, near Kabul, M. Hackin discovered a remarkable image of Sūrya, dressed like a Sassanian king and wearing a round apron-like tunic fringed with pearls[14] set in the dress. The Sassanian kings had a special liking for pearls. Bāṇa also refers to the fashion of pearl-spangled tunics worn by kings in the train of Harṣa. Some of the statues bearing close Sassanian influence lead us to infer that the intercourse between India and Persia in the Gupta — Sassanian epoch was much more intimate than is often imagined. A life-size bust (D1 Mathura Museum[15], wearing a Kulah cap Sk. kholam), with a crescent and globule symbol, spiral curls of hair, a tight beard band, a bejewelled cuirass and a belled coat, represents a figure in Sassanian style. During the reigns of Shahpur II, and his successors Ardshir II and Shahpur III (between AD 309 and 386) up to the reign of Khuśru (AD 590-628), the cultural inter-relation between India and Persia, was at its peak. The two scenes one of the so-called Persian embassy being received by an Indian King in full court ceremony, painted in Cave I at Ajanta, another scene identified as that of the Persian King Khuśru Parwiz and his beautiful queen Śirin, illustrate the degree of Sassanian influence. This is evident in all the paintings and sculptures and also in terracottas.

[13] Agarvala, V. S., *The Gupta Art,* pp. 9-10.

[14] Tāramuktāphalopacīyamāna vārabāṇa/

[15] Agarvala, V.S., *A Handbook to the Mathura Museum,* fig.11, p. 52.

The Indian artists in rendering the faces and costumes of their foreign neighbours, scored a striking amount of success.[16]

The miniatures of the Ādityas, the planets, the zodiacal signs, the seven Ṛṣis as well as the sons of the Sun-God are sometimes found represented on the image of the Sun-God.

Solar worship, as we have already seen, is as old as the Vedas but though allegorical allusions to his car, his horses, his wives are fairly common in the Vedas, the divine energy of the dazzling luminary is the object of devotion there than his more concrete form. The most sacred hymn of the Vedas, the Gāyatrī or the Savitṛ, which every Brāhmin must recite every day, is a verse addressed to the God Savitṛ. Here the divine energy of Savitṛ is prayed, for leading the intellect ever onward to higher paths. We need not stop to consider the lack of humility and the spirit of sturdy independence breathing through this noble hymn of the Rigveda, which is considered by the Brahmins as the essence of all Vedas. We are here only concerned with the fact that the Divine Energy and not the Form of the Sun-God, the most brilliant object available for contemplation to mankind, is the object of devotion. Gradually, the myths, which are already well-developed in the Vedas, began to crystallize.

All traditions point to the Āryan community at as, the people who were the first worshippers of the Sun-God. The introduction of Solar images in India, is ascribed to Sāmba, son of Lord Kṛṣṇa, who is said to have been cured of leprosy by worshipping the Sun, and thereupon to have installed a golden image of the Sun-God at Multan.

Instances of Solar worship are common from the time of the Gupta Emperors. The *Mandasor* inscription[17] of the time of Kumāra Gupta records the erection of a temple of the Sun-God in AD 437. The Indore copper plate grant of Skanda Gupta, records a grant for the maintenance of a lamp in a temple of the Sun AD 465–66. The Gwalior stone inscription of the 18th year of

[16] Agarvala, V.S., *The Gupta Art*, p. 10.
[17] Bhandarkar, R.G., *Vaiṣṇavism and Śaivism.*

Mihirakula (Fleet, pp. 1-61) records, the erection of a temple of the Sun-God.

The Vardhana Emperor[18] who followed the Guptas were staunch worshippers of the Sun-God. Their very names, such as Āditya Vardhana, Prabhākara Vardhana indicate their faith; and Emperor Harṣa expressly applies the epithet of "Paramāditya bhakta" (Great devotee of the Sun-God) to his ancestors in his copper plate inscriptions. Yuan-Chwang[19], who was present at the court of Harṣavardhana, mentions a temple of the Sun-God at Kanauj, which had 1,000 attendants attached to it.

The Shahpur stone image inscription of Ādityasen (AD 672) and the Deo Baraṇārk inscription of JivitaGupta II — his descendant, of the family of the later Gupta who succeeded the Vardhans in the Soverignty of East India, both relate to Solar worship. The innumerable images of the Sun-God that are found all over Bengal belong to a much later period and testify to the popularity of the deity even during the long period of the supremacy of the Buddhist Pāla kings. The Varmans and the Senas who followed the Pālas specifically call themselves "Saura" i.e. worshippers of the Sun-God. The Solar worship in Orissa culminated in the stupendous structures at Konaraka, which still stands on the coast of Orissa, as a mute witness to the great popularity of the Sun-God in Eastern India.

"The most famous image of the Sun-God in India was that at Multan, whose temple was visited by Yuan-Chwang. He saw there a magnificent temple of the Sun profusely decorated. The image was of cast gold. "The kings and high families of the five Indies all worship the Deva" writes this zealous Buddhist with admiration, who had hardly called the worshippers of Brahmanical faith by any other epithet than "unbelievers" all through the records of his travels."

The Sun-cult flourished throughout Northern Inda is evident from the epigraphy, iconography, temples and literature. The

[18] *Epigraphia Indica*, pp. 72-73.

[19] Beal, *Siyuki*, Vol.I. p. 223.

largest number of Sun-temples has been found in North-western and Western India. There is a continuous history of the prevalance of the Sun-cult in this region under the patronage of the Maitrakas of Gujarat, Sendrakas, Chālukyas, Kalchuris, etc.

In East India, the popularity of the Sun-cult, is attested by the large number of Sun-images as from Chandimuda, Dinajpur, Manda, Dacca, as well as by Sun-temples at Kiching[20] (Orissa) and Konaraka. Konaraka, in Orissa, was the important place of Sun-worship. The discovery of the image of Sūrya — from a number of places in Bihar and the existence of the old Sun-temple of Kandahar, of Narsimhadeva's time (13th cent. AD) prove the existence of Sun-cult in Bihar. Thus the whole of Northern India was under the impact of the Sun-cult. The Sun-worship of the northern type was quite popular in the Deccan.

The Sun-temples have been found from Gop (6th Cent.), Visāvāda, Sūtrapādā and Thān (7th–8th cent.), Kinderkheda, Pasthar (10th cent.) Modhera, Hiraṇya, Somanātha and Thān (AD 950–1300) — all in Gujarat's Kathiawad region. The other regions of Western India as Rajasthan and Punjab were also under strong impact of the Sun-cult. Multan in Punjab continued to be a stronghold of the Sun-cult as is evidenced by Hiuen-Tsang, Alberuni and Arab writers[21]. In Rajasthan, a number of Sun-temples of this period has been discovered such as Osia, Chittorgarh, Sirohi, Bharatpur, Tusa, etc. Sun-worship was popular in Rajasthan during the period from AD 600 – 1400. The Sun-cult was well established in the early mediaeval period in Kashmir, is well attested by the Mārtaṇḍa temple of Kashmir (8th cent. AD).

Thus the geographical extension of Sun-worship was not confined to Western and North-western India. It spread to the Gangetic Doab, Central India and Eastern India as well. The prevalence of the Sun-cult in Central India is attested by the epigraphy, monuments, images and literature.

---

[20] Banerjee, J.N., *Development of Hindu Iconography*, Calcutta, p. 439.

[21] Srivastava, V.C., *Sun Worship in Ancient India*, Allahabad, 1972, pp. 358-360.

The Sanskrit texts all point to Sāmba as the founder of this image. In Varāha Purāṇa (Bangabhashi edition, Chap. 177, p. 565), the story how Sāmba was cursed by his father Kṛṣṇa with leprosy, because the beauty of his person had moved the hearts of his step-mothers, is narrated at length. From a passage, there it appears that on his recovery by worshipping the Sun, he established three temples in India. One in *Udayāchala* (the mount of the Sun-rise), a second at *Madurā (Mathura?)* and the third at *Sāmbapura,* representing, respectively, the morning, the midday and the evening sun. Udayāchala may be the same as Udayagiri, midway between Cuttack and Puri in Orissa. The Arka Kshetra or the zone of the Sun in Orissa, which includes the locality of the temple of the Sun at Konaraka, is well-known and is claimed in Kapila saṁhitā (which seems a later work) as the original place of Sāmba's austerities[22]. The worship of Jagannath at Puri, is also supposed by some[23] to be connected with Solar worship, and the image itself is supposed to be a primitive representation of the orb of the Sun. It is noteworthy that the Car festival (Ratha Yātrā) of Jagannātha at Puri is a feature which was also observed in the worship of the Sun-God images at Mathura and Sāmbapura and Varāha Purāṇa extols the merit accruing to the pilgrims, who, having attended the Car festival of the Sun-God at Mathura, also attend the same festival held in honour of the Sun at Sāmbapura, which was held on the Saptami Tīthī in the month of Māgha.

Sāmbapura is without any doubt the present Multan. Bhaviṣya Purāna (Chap. 74) states that it stood on the Chandrabhaga river, one of the five branches of the Indus. The Chandrabhāgā[24] is the modern Chenab on banks of which stands Multan. But the identity of Multan and Sāmbapura is placed beyond

---

[22] Ganguli, *Orissa and Her Remains,* pp. 439-41.

[23] Bloch, *Supplementary Catalogue of the Archaeological Collections in the Indian Museum,* Section – Images of the Sun-God.

[24] "It may be noted that Konaraka also stands on a small stream called Chandrabhāgā and this fact must have easily lent to the clever fake of Kapila Saṁhitā in making it the original place where Sāmba established the image of the Sun-God.

doubt by the following observation of Alberuni.[25]

Utpala, a native of Kashmir, says, in his commentary in the Saṁhitā regarding this subject, "The names of countries change and particularly in the Yugas. So, Multan was originally called Kaśyapapura, then Haṁsapura, then Bagapura, then Sāmbapura and then Mūlasthāna, i.e. the original place."

That the Car festival at Sāmbapura was no myth, and had an all-India renown, is evident from the following passage in Alberuni (Vol. II, p. 184).

"The Hindus of Multan have a festival which is called "Sāmbapura Yātrā". They celebrate it in honour of Sun-God and worship him." From astronomical calculations given after this to show, how the exact date of the festival is determined on the almanacs it, appears, that it had a permanent place in the almanacs of the period."

The figure of the Sun-God of Multan appears on three coins (circa AD 500) illustrated by Cunningham in Vol. V of his Archaeological Survey Reports on Pl. XXXVII. Only the bust of the God appears on the coins, which shows him as a rayed God wearing armour.

The golden image, which Yuan-Chwang saw, may have been the original image, established at Sāmbapura. It was destroyed by Muhammad bin Kasim. It appears to have been 230 maunds in weight.[26]

A fresh image appears to have been installed after this sacrilege for Alberuni describes the image (Vol. I, p. 116) is of wood covered by leather. It appears[27] that this image continued to exist down to the 17th century, when it is said to have been finally destroyed by Aurangzeb.

We can conclude after the classification of the images that the number of horses in early images, is four in number as we have the description of the Sun in Vedas. Thus in Mathura,

---

[25] Vol.I, p. 298.

[26] *History of India by its Own Historians*, Vol.1, p. 206.

[27] Cunningham, *Archaeological Survey Report*, Vol.V, p. 119.

Bodhagaya, Bhājā we have four horses and in later images we have seven horses either representing the seven days of the week or seven metres.

Another interesting point to note is the chariot as well as horses. In early works the chariot is big, while in later works we usually find smaller chariots. Sometimes we find the miniature horses in the pedestal, but no sign of the chariot.

In all the sculptures (early or late), we find the chariot in front but only in Bhājā we have its position in the side. In old images generally, we find only Daṇḍa and Piñgala, but later images are closely surrounded by a big group. The Kiriṭa of the Sun, is richly ornamented in late images. Thus we see the richness of the ornaments which we miss in early images.

Moreover, the South Indian figures of Sūrya have, as a rule, their hands lifted up as high as the shoulders, and are made to hold lotus flowers which are only half blossomed, the images have invariably the Udarabandha and their legs and feet are always left bare. The North Indian images, on the other hand, have generally their hands at the natural level of the hips or the elbows and are made to carry full-blown lotuses which rise upto the level of the shoulders and their forelegs have coverings resembling boots. The Udarabandha is not found in the northern variety of the images of the Sun-God, but there is a thin cloth or a sort of coat of mail shown as being worn on the body. The South Indian images are often with the seven horses and their driver Aruṇa, those which belong to the extreme south of South India, to such parts as the Tamil districts, do not possess any attendant deities like Daṇḍa, Piñgala and the goddesses. The images of the Sun-God as found in the Karṇāṭadeśa and the Southern Mahratta country, corresponding roughly to the ancient Chalukya and Hoyaṣalā kingdoms, have invariably two goddesses sculptured one on each side of Sūrya. The common features, of both southern and northern varieties of Sūrya, are that the head is in all cases adorned with a Kiriṭa surrounded by a circular halo or Prabhāmaṇḍala, and that in several instances the characteristic seven horses and their driver Aruṇa are not missing.

APPENDIX I

Image of Sūrya	Position	Headdress	Horses	Assistants	Lotus	Boots	Other Symbols
Mathura 0/3/23/1 (Musée Guimet)	Standing	Kiriṭa-mukuṭa	—	—	Lotus(?)	Boots	—
13123/19 (Musée Guimet)	Bust	”	—	—	Lotus(?)	—	—
13123/1 (Musée Guimet)	Seated(?)	Like a chignon in the centre	4	—	—	Not visible	There is a Solar disc behind him. The horses are on both the sides. Things in the hands are not clear.
13123/20 (at Boston)	Seated	—	—		—	—	—
Bodhagaya 115/23 (Musée Guimet)	Standing (?)	Like a chignon in the centre	4	Uṣā and Pratyuṣā with bows and arrows; Daṇḍa and Piñgala on both the sides (?).	—	—	The position of the horses is the same as in the Mathura type. Sūrya has a chatra. The object in one of the hands is not clear.

Image of Sūrya	Position	Headdress	Horses	Assistants	Lotus	Boots	Other Symbols
Bhājā L'Inde et l'orient Classique Par G. Combaz	Seated	Headdress with a chignon in the middle.	4	With two women (perhaps wives) with chatra and chāmara.	—	—	Sūrya holds reins in the hands. There are four horses but the chariot is not seen in front. The chariot has two wheels. The demon is under the chariot.
Gréco-Buddhist Kabul (5th or 6th cent.) Pl. 136	Seated (with legs raised)	Headdress of Kabul type.	2 Other two are not visible due to the front ones.	Daṇḍa and Piñgala; Aruṇa.	Hands are broken. So nothing is visible.	Boots	This type of seated posture resembles the seated Sūrya type of Mathura (but the style is distinctly late-Hellenistic of Gāndhāra region).
Gāndhāra (Palmyra) Pl.135	Seated	Not visible (head is damaged).	2	One is visible and the other is nearly damaged.	?	?	Behind the head there is one lunar arc. It is called Candra. Position of the horses is similar to that of the Sun-image at Kabul.
Garhwā (Allahabad) Pl. 130	Seated	Style of Kabul	3 (other four are not visible)	Uṣā and Pratyuṣā	Not clear perhaps, half-blown lotus.	?	The position of the side horses is like that of the Kabul image but the middle one looks like galloping.

Image of Sūrya	Position	Headdress	Horses	Assistants	Lotus	Boots	Other Symbols
Peshawar Pl. 135	Standing	As in Bhumarā (high head-dress).	—	May be Daṇḍa and Piñgala	—	Boots	The figures of the assistants are not complete. One has a circular disc – behind the head other has semi-circular or a lunar disc. The dress of the central figure is like a Bhumarā type.
Gupta or post-Gupta *Ellora* 141224/18 (Musée Guimet)	Standing	With three knots.	7	With Uṣā and Pratyuṣā, holding bows and arrows and with Aruṇa as charioteer.	Half-blown lotuses. The hands are lifted up to the level of the shoulder.	Not visible	The chariot has two wheels.
Bhumarā 141224/2 (Musée Guimet)	Standing	Long but flat at the top.	—	Daṇḍa and Pinñgala (Both have their coiffure pointed at the top).	Half-blown Lotus(?).	Boots	Something not clear in the hands. The dress is nearly the same as in 013123/2(?) Mathura but slight difference in the shape of the crown and the dress is rather shorter than that of Mathura as above.
Khaṇḍagiri 1342/20 (Musée Guimet)	Seated	—	—	—	—		Not clear.

Image of Sūrya	Position	Headdress	Horses	Assistants	Lotus	Boots	Other Symbols
Ellorā Ellorā cave temples (Burgess. 1883) A.S. Of India, Lank-eśvara, fig.1, p. XXX	Standing	Kiriṭa-mukuta	—	Two wives holding flowers in the hands. Piñgala and Daṇḍa as usual with their weapons, but the place of these seems to be inter-changed.	Lotus	Boots	Here the dress of the Sun is not like the northerners, but he is with boots. The dress of Piñgala is somewhat long, cov-ering up to the feet, as said in Bṛhatsaṁhitā.
Rājashahi Dis-trict A.S.I.; An-nual Reports (1908-09), Fig.3, 8th cent. A.D. from Nimatpura, in the Rājashahi district.	Standing	low cap	—	Daṇḍa and Piñgala	Full-blown lotuses.	Boots	Draped in long tunics, fastened at the waist with a string belt (like Bhumarā or Peshawar type).
Madras Presi-dency Pl. LXXXVI, Gudimal-lam (anterior to 7th cent. A.D.) (Elements of *Hindu Iconogra-phy*, Vol.1, G. Rao).	Standing	Not very high headdress	—	—	not clear.	—	With upavīta – the hands are lifted up to the level of the shoulders.

Image of Sūrya	Position	Headdress	Horses	Assistants	Lotus	Boots	Other Symbols
Melcheri Pl. LXXXVII, near Kāveripakkam (late Pallava period, i.e. AD 800 *(E of H. Iconography,* Vol. 1, G. Rao)	Standing	High head-dress	7 (not very clear)	Aruṇa (charioteer)	Hands are broken.	—	—
Mediaeval Pl. XCI, Dharwar District (Cha-lukya—Hoyaśalā Country) (South Indian variety) (*E. of H. Iconography,* Vol. 1, G. Rao)	Standing	Kiriṭa-mukuṭa.	7(with-out Aruṇa)	Rājñī and Nikṣubhā (with cāmaras in the hands).	Half-blown lotuses. The hands of Sūrya are lifted up to the level of shoulders.	—	Udarabandha and Avyanga. On the top there is Kīrtimukha. Sūrya is surrounded by the flames (or rays). The hands are broken.
Kanthkot pl. LXV, fig. 1 (10th cent. ?, *A.S. of W. India,* Burgess, 1876)	Standing	Kiriṭa-cylindrical. Daṇḍa with conical cap; Piñgala with turban; two women having coiffure like a knot in the middle.	—	Daṇḍa and Pinñgala (as usual). Two women with Kaṭihasta.	Two full-blown lotuses.	Boots	Hands are broken. Sūrya has a maṇḍala behind his head in the shape of a lotus petals. One cloth is hanging from the hands in the form of a garland.

Image of Sūrya	Position	Headdress	Horses	Assistants	Lotus	Boots	Other Symbols
Nuggehall pl. XCII (South Indian variety), (Ibid.)	Standing	Kirīṭa-mukuṭa	7 with Aruṇa	Uṣā & Pratyuṣa with bows and arrows. Besides these a number of small figures are carved probably to represent Daṇḍa, Piñgala and others.	Half-blown lotuses. The hands are lifted up to the level of the shoulders.	—	On the topmost tier of the sculpture, stand five figures resembling boys; perhaps these are Ṛṣis Sanaka and others. In the tier below this are a set of musicians playing upon different musical instruments.
Arasavalli, pl. LXV, fig. 2 (10th cent.?) (Burgess, 1876).	Standing	Headdress with precious stones	7	Two lokapālas with swords and shields raised. Two male figures with bows and arrows. One female figure near the feet of god (earth goddess). Aruṇa, a charioteer on the middle horse.	Lotus as well as buds in his two hands.	—	Sūrya-maṇḍala, richly ornamented. Kirtimukha on the top of the pilaster. Two Gandharvas with the chāmara on both the sides of the head. Sūrya as well as all other figures are with Tilaka mark on the forehead. Sūrya has a round mark and his assistants have the Urdhvapuṇḍra mark. All are dressed in dhotī. Sūrya is with moustache (South Indian Type).

Image of Sūrya	Position	Headdress	Horses	Assistants	Lotus	Boots	Other Symbols
Arasavalli pl. LXV, fig. 3 (bronze image 10th cent.?) (Burgess, 1876)	Standing	Headdress with diadems	—	Two women holding in their right hands lotus buds. They are dressed in sarees and with head-dress.	Two hands have lotuses and other two are in Kaṭihasta and Abhaya pose.	—	Sūrya with Tilaka on the fore-head. Women are in profile. So, the sign on the forehead is not visible. Kīrtimukha is on the head of Sūrya. Sūrya is dressed in Dhotī (South Indian type).
Modherā pl. LVI, fig. 5 (*A.Survey of North Gujarat*— (Burgess and Cousens, 1902)	Standing	Highly decorated headdress	7	The standing figures, having animal faces — perhaps his sons — Aśvinīs, Two male figures are seated, one with Daṇḍa and other is not clear. Above these two figures are seated cross-legged.	Two full blown lotuses.	Boots	On both sides of the Sūrya's head, there are two Gandharvās with garlands — hands are broken.
Pl. LVI, fig. 6 (Burgess and Cousens).	Standing	Headdress with ornaments		Daṇḍa and Piñgala.	Two full-blown lotuses.	Boots	Two figures on both sides are in Abhaya pose.

Image of Sūrya	Position	Headdress	Horses	Assistants	Lotus	Boots	Other Symbols
Koṇāraka fig. 160 (11–12th cent. AD), A.S. of India of Bihar and Orissa, Kuraishi, 1932	Standing	With Kiriṭa	7	Daṇḍa and Piñgala Two Women holding flowers, charioteer Aruṇa is there.	Two full blown-lotuses (hands are broken).	Boots	Kīrtimukha (on the head of Sun-God).
Koṇāraka Pl. LXVII, fig. 220 (*History of Indian and Indonesian Art* by A.K. Coomaraswamy Sūrya Deul wheel detail)	Seated	With Kiriṭa	1	—	—	Boots	Here, Sūrya is seated on a horse. He holds spear in his hands and pierces in the body of the devils. (This is the unique figure of Sūrya. It is exactly the same as described in Agni Purāṇa).
Bhuvaneśvara Pl. XV. (J. of Oriental Art, Vaital Deval Temple)	Standing	Jewelled Crown	7	Uṣā, Pratyuṣā and Aruṇa.	Two full-blown lotuses.	Not visible	Two Gandharvās with the garlands on both sides of Sūrya.

Image of Sūrya	Position	Headdress	Horses	Assistants	Lotus	Boots	Other Symbols
Pl. LXXI, fig. 227, Chapra (11th cent.), Rajashahi Museum – Ibid	Standing	With pointed head-dress	7	Daṇḍa and Piñgala, Rājñi & Nikṣubhī, Aruṇa and Pṛthvī	Full-blown lotus.	Boots	Kīrtimukha – two Gandharvās on both sides with garlands.
Pl. XCIV, fig. 1, Belur, Sūrya-Nārāyaṇa Hoyaṣala Country E.H. Iconography, Vol. 1 (G. Rao)	Standing	Kiriṭa-mukuṭa	7	Aruṇa - charioteer	Two hands carry lotuses and two carry Śankha and Cakra.	?	With Udarabandha and Aviyañga; Figure with Four hands.
Pl. LXXXVIII, fig. 3, Rūpanagar Krishnagarh district, Rājputānā Marble (G. Rao)	Seated	Perhaps Karaṇḍa-mukuṭa	7	Aruṇa	Two hands carry full-blown lotuses and in two Kamaṇḍalu and Akṣamālā.	—	The chariot has two wheels. Sūrya is seated cross-legged. His face is straight and the horses and Aruṇa are on the sides. It is doubtful to consider this figure as an image of Sun-God.

Image of Sūrya	Position	Headdress	Horses	Assistants	Lotus	Boots	Other Symbols
Pl. XCIII fig. 2, (Ajmer Rājputānā Museum) North Indian type (G. Rao)	Standing	Conical shape	7	Daṇḍa and Piñgala; Rājñī Nikṣubhā, Prithvi and Aruṇa	Full-blown lotuses above the level of shoulders.	Boots	Gandharvās on both sides of the Sūrya.
Pl. LXXXIX, Chitorgarh, Marwar (G. Rao)	Seated cross-legged	Karaṇḍa-mukuṭa	7	Four wives; Daṇḍa and Piñgala, Aruṇa	Full blown lotus in one hand and the other hand is broken.	—	The head is destroyed.
Pl. XC(fig. 1) Ajmer-Rajputānā Museum (G. Rao)	Standing	Kiriṭa-mukuṭa, with a flat top	—	Rājñi and Nikṣubhā; Daṇḍa and Piñgala	With two full-blown lotuses, hands are on the hips.	Boots	Aśvini devatās, with horse faces, are seated cross-legged in the niches near the head of Sūrya on both the sides.Here, Sūrya has a very broad belt.
Pl. XC, fig. 2 Ajmer-Rajputānā Museum (G. Rao)	Standing	Kiriṭa-mukuṭa, with a flat top	7	Rājñi and Nikṣubhā; Uṣā and Pratyuṣā	Two full blown lotuses up to the level of shoulders, hands near the hips.	Boots	Sūrya with broad belt.

Image of Sūrya	Position	Headdress	Horses	Assistants	Lotus	Boots	Other Symbols
Pl. XC, fig. 3 (G. Rao)	Standing	Kiriṭa-mukuṭa, with a flat-top	—	Daṇḍa, Piñgala; two Aśvini Kumāras; Uṣā and Pratyuṣā near Kāntimaṇḍala.	Full-blown lotuses — one hand is broken.	Boots	Sūrya has put on a very thin cloth; a narrow belt, encircling the waist.
Pl. XCV, Junāgaḍha Museum (*Toraṇa of a Sūrya temple* (G. Rao)	Seated	Kiriṭa-mukuṭa	7	Uṣā and Pratyuṣā.	Full-blown lotuses.	—	Twelve Ādityas are sculptured in this Toraṇa; some of them are with two and others with four goddesses. All are standing, except the central figure.
Pl. XCIII, fig. 1, (South Indian variety and belongs to Tamil Country - G. Rao)	Standing	High head-dress	—	—	Half-blown lotuses; hands are up to the loins.	—	—
Pl. XCIV fig. 2, (Madras Museum South Indian type- Tamil Country) (G. Rao)	Standing	Kiriṭa-mukuṭa	—	—	Half-blown lotuses. Hands up to the level of loins.	—	Udarabandha and Aviyānga.

Image of Sūrya	Position	Headdress	Horses	Assistants	Lotus	Boots	Other Symbols
Pl. LXXXVIII, fig. 1, Madras Museum – Bronze (G. Rao)	Seated cross-legged	Karaṇḍa-mukuṭa	7	Two women – one with chatra and other with chāmara, Aruṇa – charioteer.	Lotus (Buds?).	—	Kīrtimukha above the head of Sūrya.
141162/6 (Musée Guimet), Bronze (Nālandā-Patna district)	Standing	Kiriṭa-mukuṭa	—	Daṇḍa and Piñgala.	Full-blown lotuses.	Boots	Sword hanging on the right side of the Sun.
15459/1 (Musée Guimet), Kuruvati, Bellary district (South India)	Standing	Kiriṭa-mukuṭa	—	Rājñī and Nikṣubhā.	Full-blown lotuses.	—	Upavīta and Udarabandha, Sūrya is under Śeṣanāga (form of Sūrya-Nārāyaṇa).
15242/22 (Musée Guimet) Kumbha Koṇam, Tanjore District	Standing	Kiriṭa-mukuṭa	—	—	Half-blown lotuses.	—	There is one Solar disc behind Sūrya; he has Udarabandha and a Upavīta.

Image of Sūrya	Position	Headdress	Horses	Assistants	Lotus	Boots	Other Symbols
14611/2 (Musée Guimet) Trichinapoly	Standing	Kiriṭa-mukuṭa	—	Bṛahmā and Śiva; Aśvini devatās?	Lotus	—	Here Sūrya has three faces and four hands. He carries Śaṅkha and Padma. One hand is in Kaṭihasta and the fourth one is not clear but may be in Abhaya Mudrā. There are Kinnaris behind the Sūrya.
15221/34 (Musée Guimet) Chidambaram (South India)	Standing	Kiriṭa-mukuṭa	7	Rājñī and Nikṣubhā; Aruṇa.	Lotus	—	Here Sūrya has three faces and six hands. He carries in two hands Śankha and lotus. Two hands are in Abhaya and Varada poses. The objects in two hands are not clear. Here the charioteer Aruṇa is shown with legs. Sūrya has udarabandha as well as upavīta.
Ḍākā (Mūrtivijnāna) - Khare Pl. LIX	Standing	Kiriṭa-mukuṭa	7	Daṇḍa, Piñgala; two wives with chāmara. Uṣā and Pratyuṣā with bows and arrows; Aruṇa; Aśvini-kumāras with horse-faces.	Full-blown lotus	Boots	Two hands are broken. Kīrtimukha over the head of Sūrya. Two Gandharvās with the garlands.

Image of Sūrya	Position	Headdress	Horses	Assistants	Lotus	Boots	Other Symbols
Sundia (in Bengal, 9th cent. ?), Annual Reports, A.S. of India – 1922-23 pl. XXXVII, a.	Standing	Well ornamented mukuṭa	7	Daṇḍa and Piñgala; Uṣā and Pratyuṣā.	Full-blown lotus.	Boots	Something like a sword is hanging on the left side of the central figure (Sūrya).
Fig. 3, copper image from near Mangalabārī District – Dinājpura (Annual Report of the Varendra Research Society, 1927-28)	Seated	Conical mukuṭa	7	—	Two full-blown lotuses, one hand in Varada mudrā and the other in Abhaya mudrā.	—	Sūrya with four hands. He is dressed in dhotī. The representation of the Sun-God with four hands agrees with the Dhyāna mudrā in the Tantrasāra.
Pl. 1, from Mahendra, District Dinajpur (Bengal) Annual Report of the Varendra Research Society. 1932-33 and 1933-34	Standing	Conical mukuṭa	7	Daṇḍa, Piñgala; Uṣā and Pratyuṣā, Aruṇa, Prithvī, Samjñā Nikṣubhā.	Two full-blown lotuses Akṣamālā, Kamaṇḍalu, Varada and Abhaya Mudrā.	Boots	Sūrya with six hands, as in the Viśvakarma Śāstra, Sūrya is enumerated as an Āditya with four hands, with attributes as follows: Akṣamālā, Kamaṇḍalu and two lotuses. On both sides of the Sun, are two Gandharvās with garlands. On the top is the Kīrtimukha, and Sūrya has a Prabhāmaṇḍala.

Image of Sūrya	Position	Headdress	Horses	Assistants	Lotus	Boots	Other Symbols
Fig. 1, District Bogra; Annual Report of the Varendra Research Society 1926-27	Standing	Cap like Kiriṭa.	7	Daṇḍa, Piñgala; Uṣā and Pratyuṣā and Aruṇa.	Full-blown lotus.	Not visible.	He has a circular halo round his head. He has a short neck-lace apparently of beads. The sacred thread so prominent in later Sūrya images, is absent in this figure. Along his left side is seen hanging a sword, kept in a position by means of a chain. The wheel of the chariot is depicted in the middle of the pedestal. The lower part of the body is clad in a short skirt, tied round the waist by a girdle terminating above the boots, and the upper half is covered with a coat of mail (udīcya dress or the dress of a north-erner).

Appendix II

INSCRIPTIONS

1. THE INSCRIPTION OF MANDASOR (AD 437–38 AND AD 473–74) FOR THE ERECTION OF THE SUN TEMPLE.

"While he, the noble Bandhuvarman, the best of kings, the strong shouldered one, was governing this city of Daśapura, which had been brought to a state of great prosperity, a noble (and) unequalled temple of the bright-rayed (Sun), was caused to be built by the silk-cloth weavers, as a guild, with the stores of wealth acquired by (the exercise of their) craft, (a temple) which, having broad and lofty spires, (and) resembling a mountain, and white as the mass of the rays of the risen moon, shines, charming to the eye, having the similarity of (being) the lovely crest-jewel, fixed (in its proper place, of (this) city of the west.

And, in the course of a long time, under other kings, part of this temple fell into disrepair, so now, in order to increase their own fame, the whole of this most noble house of the Sun has been repaired again by the munificent corporation... by the command of the guild and from devotion. (This) temple of the sun was caused to built...."

L. 16 Smri (Smṛi) tvā yam = adyāpy = ari Sundarīṇām/ bhayādbhavaty = āyata locanānām ghanastan-āyāsakaraḥ prakampaḥ Tasminn = eva kshitipati-Vri (vṛi) she Bamdhuvarmmaṇya = udare samyak-sphitaṃ Daśapuram-idam pālayaty = unnat-āṁśe Śilpāvāptair = ddahana-Samudayaiḥ paṭṭavāyair = Udāram Śreṇibhūtair = bbhavanam = atulam kāritam

L. 17 dīpta-raṣmiḥ Vistīrṇṇa-tuṅga śikharaṁ ṣikharī prakāśam = abhyudgat = endu-amalaraśmi-kalāpa-gauram....

L. 19 Stana-jaghan-ghan-ālingana-nirbhartsita-tuhina-hima-pāte Mālavāṇāṃ gaṇa-sthityā Yāt[e] śatacatuṣṭaye tri-na-vaty-adhike-bdānām = ri(ṛi) tau sevya = ghana-svane Sahasya-māsa-śuklasya praśaste = hni trayodaśe

Maṅgala-ācāra-vidhinā prāsādo = yaṁ nive-sitah Bahunā Samatitena.

L. 20 Kālen = ānyaiśca pārtthivaiḥ vyāśiryyat = aikadeṣo = sya bhavanasya tato-dhunā Sva-yaṣo-V[r]i(vṛi) ddhaye sarvvam = aty-udāra m = udarāyā Saṁskāritam = idam bhūyaḥ śreṇyā bhānumatogṛhaṃ Atyunnatam = avadātam nabha [ḥ] spṛśanna = iva manoharaiḥ śikharaiḥ

L. 23 .....Śreṇy-ādeśena bhaktyā ca kāritaṃ bhavanam raveḥ/ Pūrvā c = eyam prayatnena racitā Vatsabhaṭṭinā

2. THE INDORE COPPER-PLATE INSCRIPTION (AD 464) OF SKANDAGUPTA

"The Brahmin Devaviṣṇu who belongs to the community of Chaturvedi of Padma of the town Candrapura — who is the son of Deva and the grandson of Haritrāta (and) the son of the son's son of Ḍuḍika, who always recites the hymns of the Agnihotra sacrifice, who belongs to the Rāṇāyaniya (śākhā); and who is of the Varshagaṇa gotra for the increase of his own fame he gives a donation (of which the interest is) to be applied to (the maintenance of) a lamp for the divine Sun, which has been established (in a temple) by the Kṣatriyas."

L. 5 Sāmānya-brāhmaṇa-Devavishṇur = devaputro Haritrāta-Pauttraḥ.....(L. 7) adhishlā (shṭhā) nasya prācyām diṣ-Indrapur-adhishlāna-mādāsyātalagnam-eva pratishṭhāpitaka-bhagavate savitre dīp-opayojyam-ātma-yaṣobhirṛddhye mūlyam prayacchatiḥ

3. GWALIOR STONE INSCRIPTION OF MIHIRAKULA (6TH CENT.)

".....Who is renowned under the name of Mihirakula, (and) who, (himself) unbroken, (broke the power of Paṣupati, ...On the delightful mountain which is specked with various metals and has the appellation of Gopa, a stone-temple, the chief among the best of temples, of the sun, for the purpose of increasing the religious merit of (his) parents and of himself, and of whose who, by the..... of the king, dwell on this best of mountains.....

Those who cause to be made an excellent house of the Sun, like in lustre to the rays of the moon — their abode is in heaven, until the destruction of all things. (This) very famous proclamation of the true religion has been composed through devotion to the sun, by him, who is renowned by the name of Keśava and by ......ditya."

L. 3 Tasy = odita-kula-Kīrtteḥ putro = tula Vikramaḥ patiḥ Pṛthvyāḥ Mihirakula-etikhyāto = bhango Yaḥ paśupatim (...)/

L. 6 Nānā-dhātu-vichitre Gop-āhvaya-nāmni bhūdhare ramye kāritvān = śailamayam bhanoḥ praśadavara — mukhyam//

L. 7 Ye kārayanti bhānoś-chandra-āṁṣu-samaprabham gṛha-pravaram teshām vāsaḥ Svargge yāvatkalpa-Kṣayo bhavati// Bhaktyā raver = vviracitāni Saddharmma-khyāpanam su-kīrtimayam nāmnā ca Keśaveti-prathitena Ca//

L. 8 ....di (?) tyena

4. COPPER SEAL INSCRIPTION OF HARSHAVARDHANA

"...the most devout worshipper of the Sun, the Mahārāja, the illustrious Rājyavardhana (1). His son, (who meditated on) his feet, (was) (the most devout) worshipper of the Sun, the Mahārāja, the illustrious Ādityavardhana (begotten) on the illustrious Mahādevī (?). His son, who meditated on his feet (was)... the most devout worshipper of the Sun, the Paramabhaṭṭāraka and Mahārājadhirāja, the glorious Prabhākaravardhana, begotten on the Devī, (the illustrious) Mahāsenaguptā... (and) who was employed in regulating all the castes and stages of religious life. His son, who meditated on his feet (was) the most devout follower of Sugata, the Paramabhaṭṭāraka and Mahārājādhirāja, the glorious Rājyavardhana, begotten on... the glorious Yaśomati. (His younger brother), who meditated on (his feet), (is)... (the Paramabhaṭṭāraka and) Mahārājādhirāja, the glorious Harshavardhana, (begotten) on the Mahādevī, Yaśomati."

L.1 ...Y ...Śrīma (?) ha (?.dā)...

L.2 ...Paramādityabha (kta.. Mahārā)ja-Śri Rājyavardhanaḥ Tasya puttras.....tat....p (ā)
L.3 (d-ānudhyātaḥ) Śrī (?) Mahādevyām = (utpannaḥ Paramā) dityabhakto mahārāja....śrīmad- Āditya
L.4 (Varddhanaḥ) (Ta) sya (Puttras-tat-pād-ānudhyātaḥ Śrī) Mahāsenaguptā devyām-utpanna...
L.5 -. Y-Sarva(va) varṇṇ-āśrama-Vyavasthāpanapravrī-
L.6 (ttaḥ)... Y .. Va(?) Prava(r)ddha.... Paramāditya bhaktaḥ Paramabhaṭṭāraka
L.7 Mahārājādhirājo..Śrī-Prabhākaravardhanaḥ (//).....

5. GOVINDPUR INSCRIPTION (AD 1137-38)

"Hail to that gem of the three worlds, the divine Aruṇa, whose presence sanctifies the milk-ocean encircled Śakadwipa, where the Brāhmaṇas are named Magas! There is a race of twice born (sprung) from the Sun's own body, ground by the wheel, whom Sāmba himself brought hither. Glorious are they honoured in the world."

Text: Devo Jiyāt trilokī maṇirayamaruṇo-Yannivā-sena Puṇyaḥ Sākadvīpaśca dugdhāmbunidhivalayito Yatravipre magākhyā // Vaṁśastatra dvijānām bhrami-likhitanor bhāsvataḥ svāṅga (Muktaḥ) Sāmbo Yānani-naya Svayamiha mahitāste jagatyāṁ jayanti/

6. SHAHPUR STONE IMAGE INSCRIPTION OF ĀDITYASENA (AD 672-73)

"The inscription is on the pedestal of a standing image of the Sun — represented as a man, holding a water lily in each hand; and with, on each side, a small standing figure, which was found on a mound in the lands of this village.... has been granted to endure for the same time with... and the moon and the earth.

Oṁ the year 60 and 6, (the month) Mārga; the bright fortnight; the day 7 (?) on this (lunar day) (specified) as above by the day and month of the year .... in the kingdom of Śrī Ādityasena (Deva)"...

Text: Candra-kshiti-kālam-yāvat-p(r)ati-pāditam// Oṁ

Saṁvat 60, 6 Mārge ṣudi 7(?) asyāndivasa-māsa Saṁvatsar-ānupurvyām śrī-Ādityasena (deva) rāj(ye) Nālanḍa (?) Mahāgrahāre sādh(un) ā va (ba) lā dhikṛta sālopaksheṇa de(ya) dharmoyaṃ pratiṣṭhitaṃ (ḥ)

7. DEO-BARAṆĀRK (SHAHABAD DISTRICT, BIHAR) INSCRIPTION OF JIVITAGUPTA II (AD 7TH cent.)

"....Parama Maheśvara, the glorious Devaguptadeva begotten on the Paramabhaṭṭārikā, the queen Mahādevī, the glorious Koṇadevī.

By the Bhojaka Sūryamitra, belonging (to the establishment of) the divine (god) the sacred Varuṇavāsin, who was requested.... the above mentioned (village)... together with... and the village etc.; was formerly bestowed by the Parameśvara, the glorious Bālādityadeva, by (his) own charter.... the divine (god) the holy and sacred Varuṇa-Vāsin — by restoration to the Bhojaka Haṁsamitra, and by those...."

Text

Line 3/4 Paramamaheśvara Paramabhaṭṭāraka mahār(ā)j(ā)-(dhirāja.. Parameśvara) Śrī D(e)vagupta d(e)vastasya.-

Line 12/13 .... Vijnapita-Śrī Varuṇavāsi bhaṭṭāraka prati(va) (b)ddha.. bhojaka.. Sūryamittreṇa upari likhi (ta).. grāmādi... Samyutam parameśvara (Śrī(vā) (bā) lāditya devena Sva-śāsanena bhagavaśrī Varuṇavāsi-bhaṭṭāraka —.

NOTES

Inscription No. 1
See *Indian Antiquary*, 1886 p. 198.
Inscription No. 2
See Fleet, *Inscriptions of the Early Gupta Kings*, pp. 70-71.
Inscription No. 3
See Ibid., pp. 161-62.
Inscription No. 4
See Ibid., p. 231.

Inscription No. 5
See Hodivala, *Parsis of Ancient India*, p. 78.
Inscription No. 6
See Fleet, *Inscriptions of the Early Gupta Kings*, pp. 208-10.
See also *Archaeological Survey of India*, Vol.XV, 1882, p. 12.
Inscription No. 7
See Fleet, *Inscriptions of the Early Gupta Kings*, p. 213.

APPENDIX III

Some important Sun temples and images in Gujarat

SUN TEMPLES

Gop, Visāvādā, Dhānka, Bagavadara (Prācī), Khambhāta, Kaṇtha Koṭa, Koṭyarka, Moḍherā, Sanḍera, Pātaṇa, Siddhapura Baroda, Dabhoi, Pāwāgaḍha, Kāvī, Dwārkā, Piṭhadia, Varavāḍā, Kinderkhedā, Pāstar, Sutrapāḍā, Thān, Bhīmanātha (Sūrya Nārāyaṇa).

SUN IMAGES

Unā (Saurāṣṭra), Dwārkā, Junāgaḍha, Kanthakoṭa (Kaccha), Asaravalli (Kaccha), Māngrol, Ghumalī, Pāṭaṇa, Rājkot Museum, Jamnagar Museum, Baroda Museum, and Prabhāsa Pāṭan Museum, Raṇu pipalī (Dist. Baroda), Vaḍanagara, Kherāḷu, Vadodarā, Ahmadāvāda (Nilakaṇṭha Mahādeva), Māṇḍavagaḍha, Māṇḍala, Nagarā, (Khambhat) Pāncāvāḍa, Kāravaṇa, Vāvaḍi, Thān, Saptadhāreṣvara, Sutharia, Bānkhorā (Sābarakāṇthā), Vyārā, Kenyārā, Ankleśvara, Nugar, Tuṇḍāva, Aiṭhora, Piludrā (Mahesāṇā), Sarkhej (Ahmadāvāda), Garuḍeśvara (Bharucha), Sejaka (Junāgaḍha), Dāmanagar (Amreli), Dolatapar, Māṇdavī (Kaccha), Makhela (Kaccha), Śāmalāji, Ghāṭaja, Bheṭadia bhāga, Bhoḷāda (Dholakā), Pīja (Kheḍā District), Balej, Pātā, Suvan (Varvāḍā), Śrinagar, Piṇḍārā, Borichā, Akhodar, Pasanavāḍā, Khimeśvara, Roḍā, Kadvāra, Kāvi, (Jambusara), Kalsār, Śunak(?), Kotai (Kaccha), Bhāyāvadar (Temple of Somāditya), Kroḍidhvaja, Bhīmanātha (Near Prāchī Kuṇḍa), Somanāth (Sūrya-Nārāyaṇa), Ḍabhoi, Bhiloḍā (Near Iḍar), Prabhās Pāṭan (near Hiraṇya-river), Prabhas, (on banks of Triveṇi river), Dhānk, Dhamlej (Dist. Junāgaḍha), Bhetāli (Near Bhiloḍā).

BIBLIOGRAPHY

ENGLISH

Agarvala V.S., *Sculptures in the Curzon Museum of Archaeology,* Allahabad, 1939. *The Gupta Art.*

Beal, S., *Life of Hiuen Tsiang,* London, 1914. *Buddhist Records of the Western World* (Siyuki), London.

Banerjee, J.N., *Development of Hindu Iconography,* Calcutta.

Banerjee, R.D., *History of Orissa*, Calcutta, 1931. *The Temple of Śiva at Bhumrā* (Mem. A.S. of India) 16, 1924.

Bhandarkar, R.G., *Vaiṣṇavism, Śaivism and Minor Religious Systems,* Strassburg, 1913.

Bhattacharya, B., *Indian Images* Vol. 1, Calcutta, 1921.

Bloch, *Supplementary Catalogue of the Archaeological Collection of the Indian Museum,* 1911. *Cambridge Ancient History: Egypt and Babylonia,* Vol. 1, Cambridge.

Chanda — *Medieval Indian Sculptures in the British Museum,* London, 1936.

Coomaraswamy, A.K., Catalogue of the Indian Collections, Parts I & II (Museum of Fine Arts, Boston), Boston, 1923. *History of Indian and Indonesian Art,* London, 1927.

Cunningham, A., *Coins of Ancient India,* London, 1891.

Jouveau-Dubreuil, G., *Iconography of Southern India,* Paris, 1937.

Fergusson and Burgess, *The Caves and Temples of India,* London, 1880.

Fleet, *Inscriptions of the Early Gupta Kings,* (corpus inscra Ind., Vol.III), Calcutta, 1888.

Foucher, *Beginnings of Buddhist Art,* London, 1918.

Gandhi, M.K., *Autobiography of My Experiments with Truth,* Ahmedabad, 1984.

Ganguly, M., *Handbook to the Sculptures in the Museum of the Bangiya Sahitya Parishad,* Calcutta, 1922. — *Orissa and Her Remains*, Calcutta, 1912.

Ganguly, O.C., *South Indian Bronzes,* Calcutta, 1914

Grünwedel, *Buddhist Art in India* (1'edition anglaise), London, 1901.

Hastings, *Encyclopaedia of Religion and Ethics,* Vol. 7, 8, 12. *History of India by its Own historians,* Vol. 1.

Hodivala, *Parsis of Ancient India,* Bombay, 1920.

Jayswal, K.P., *Hindu Polity,* Calcutta, 1924.

Keith, *Veda of the Black Yajur School* Vol. II. Cambridge, 1914.

Kramrisch, Stella, *The Hindu Temples,* Calcutta, 1946

Majmudar, R.C., *The Vedic Age,* Calcutta, Vol. 1, 1951.

Macdonell, *Vedic Mythology,* Strassburg, 1897.

Macdonell & Keith, *Vedic Index,* London, 1912.

Müir, *Sanskrit Texts,* London, 1868-74.

Pandey, Lalita Prasad, *Sun Worship in Ancient India.*

Rao, Gopinatha, *Elements of Hindu Iconography*, Madras, 1914-15.
Sachau, *Alberuni's India*, London, 1910.
Shastri, H.K., *South Indian Images of Gods and Goddesses*, Madras, 1916.
Shrivastava, V.C., *Sun Worship in Ancient India*, 1972.
Smith V.A., *History of Fine Arts in India and Ceylon*, Oxford, 1911.
Swarupa B., *Konarka, the black Pagoda of Orissa*, Cuttack, 1910.
Vogel, J.Ph., *Catalogue of the Archaeological Museum at Mathura*, Allahabad, 1939.
Watters, *On Yuan Chwang Travels*, Vol. 1, London, 1904-05.
Whitehead, *Catalogue of the Coins in Punjab Museum*, Lahore, 1914.
Winternitz, *History of Indian Literature*, Calcutta, 1927.
Zimmer, H., *Myths and Symbols in Indian Art and Civilization*, New York, 1947.

PERIODICALS

Annual Report of the Varendra Research Society, 1926-27, 1927-28, 1932-33, 1933-34.
Archaeological Survey of India, Annual Reports, 1903-04, 1905-06, 1909-10, 1922-23, 1930-34.
Archaeological Survey of India, Annual Reports, (Burma Circle), 1922-23.
Archaeological Survey of India, Annual Reports, New Imperial Series.
Archaeological Survey of India, Annual Reports, Vol. 32,42,45,47,51.
Archaeological Survey of India, Annual Reports, North Gujarat, 1902.
Archaeological Survey of India, Annual Reports, Western Gujarat, Vol. 2, 9.
Archaeological Survey of India, Annual Reports, Western India, Vol. 2, 4, 5.
Archaeological Survey of India, Annual Reports, Mayūrbhanja, Vol. 1.
Indian Antiquary, 1880, 1886, 1909, 1925.
Indian Historical Quarterly, 1952, Vol. XXVIII.
Journal of American Oriental Society, Vol. XV 1893.
Journal of Bihar and Orissa Research Society, Vol. XIX 1933
Journal of the Indian Society of Oriental Art, Vol. XVI 1948
Journal of Royal Asiatic Society, 1908, 1909, 1916, 1917.
Marga, Vol.VI, No. 3, 1953.
Memoires of the Archaeological Survey of India (Foucher, On the Iconography of the Buddha's Nativity), No.46, 1934
Rupam Vol. VI 1921, Vol. 40, 1929.

FRENCH

Auboyer, J., *Arts et styles de l'Inde*, Paris, 1951.
Barth Auguste, *Oeuvres*, Paris, 1914-1927.
Combaz, G., *L'Inde et l'orient Classique*, Paris, 1937.
Cumont, F., *Les* Mystères *de Mithra*, Bruxells, 1913.
Contenau, G., *La Civilisation des Hittites et des Mittānniens*, Paris, 1934.
Dumezil, *Mitra et Varuṇa*, Paris, 1940.

Garnot, Fare & Jean Sainte, *Histoire générale de l'art* (Edition Flammarion), Paris, 1950.

Hackin, J., *Recherches Archaéologiques au Col de Khair Khaneh prés de Kabul* (Memoires de la délégation Archaeologique Francaise en Afghanistan), Tome VII, Paris, 1936.

Malleret, Louis, *Catalugue Général des Collections* (Musée Blanchard de la Bross, Saigon), Tome I. Hanoi, 1937.

La Vallée Poussin, Louis de, *Dynasties et Histoire de l'Inde depuis Kaniṣka,* Paris, 1935.

Vogel, J.Ph., *La Sculpture de Mathura* (Arts Asiatica Vol. XV), Paris, 1930.

Revue de Histoire des Religions, Vol.30, 1894.

GERMAN

Indische Studien, Vol.V.

Ostastiatiche Zeitschrift, Tome III.

Recht und Silte, Jolly, Strassburg, 1896.

Z.D.M.G., Vol.67.

GUJARATI

Sūryamandir Viśeṣānka, 1964

MARATHI

Khare, *Murtivijnāna,* Poona, 1939.

SANSKRIT

Adhyātma Rāmāyaṇa, Allahabad, 1913.

Agni Purāṇa, Poona, 1900.

Aitareya Āraṇyaka, Poona, 1898.

Aitareya Brāhmaṇa (Bibliotheca Indica), Calcutta, 1875-1905.

Āpastamba Dharmasūtra, Mysore, 1931.

Āśvalāyana Gṛhyasūtra (Bibliotheca Indica) Calcutta, 1869.

Bhagavadgitā, edited by Swarupananda, Almora, 1926.

Bloomfield, *Kauśiku Sūtra of the Atharvaveda*, Newhaven, 1890.

Mcdonell, *Bṛhaddevatā* (Harvard Oriental Series), 1904.

Brahmāṇḍa Purāṇa, Bombay.

Brahmavaivarta Purāṇa, poona, 1935.

Caurapancāśikā, Bombay, 1916.

Cowell, E.B., *Kauśitaki Brāhmaṇa*, Calcutta, 1861.

Egglings, *Śatapatha Brāhmaṇa* (Sacred Books of the East), Oxford, 1892-1900.

Gautama Dharmasūtra, Mysore, 1917.

Goldstücker, *Pāṇini*, London, 1861.

Hemadri, *Caturvarga Cintāmaṇi* (Bibliotheca Indica), 1873.

Keilhorn, *Mahābhāṣya* of Pātañjali, Bombay, 1880-85.

Khadiragṛhya Sūtra, Mysore, 1913.

Kumārasaṁbhava of Kālidāsa (Gujarati) Bombay, 1898.
Kūrmapurāṇa, Calcutta, 1890.
Mālati Mādhava, Bhavabhuti, Bombay, 1876.
Manusmṛti, Allahabad, 1932.
Mārkaṇḍeya Purāṇa, Calcutta, 1879.
Matsya Purāṇa, Poona, 1907.
Max Müller, *Ṛgveda*, Oxford, 1849.
Mitra, R., *Taittiriya Āraṇyaka* (Bibliotheca, Indica), Calcutta, 1872.
Nāṭyaśāstra, Varanasi, 1929.
Padmapūrāṇa, Poona, 1894.
Rādhākānta, *Śabda Kalpadruma*, Calcutta, 1821-57.
Raghunatha Śāstri, *Amarakoṣa with the Commentary of Maheśvara*, Bombay, 1896.
Raghuvaṁśa of Kālidāsa, Calcutta, 1869.
Rājataraṅgiṇi of Kalhaṇa, Bombay, 1892.
Ratnāvali of Śri Harṣa, Bombay, 1882.
Samarāngaṇa Sūtradhāra of Bhoja, Baroda, 1925.
Sāmaveda, Lahore, 1938.
Sāmbapancāṣikā, Trivendram, 1930.
Sāmbapurāṇa, Bombay.
Sānkhyāyana Brāhmaṇa, Poona.
Sāṅkhyāyana Gṛhyasūtra, Varanasi, 1908.
Saura Purāṇa, Poona, 1889.
Shama Shastri, R., *Bodhāyana Gṛhya Sūtram*, Mysore, 1920.
— *Kauṭilya Arthaśāstra,* Mysore, 1909.
Śilparatnam of Śrī Kumāra, Trivandrum, 1922.
Sūryopaniṣad, Bombay, 1923.
Taittiriya Brāhmaṇa (Bibliotheca Indica), Calcutta, 1859-62.
Taittirīya Saṁhitā, Bombay, 1945.
Vājasaneyi Samhitā, edited by Weber, Berlin, 1852.
Vālmiki Rāmāyaṇa, Calcutta, 1881-82.
Varāhamihira, *Bṛhatsaṁhitā,* Calcutta, 1865.
Varāhapurāṇa (Bibliotheca Indica), Calcutta, 1893.
Vāsavadattā of Subandhu, ed. by Hall, Calcutta, 1859.
Vāyupurāṇa, Poona, 1901.
Veṇisaṁhāra of Bhaṭṭa Nārāyaṇa, Calcutta, 1889.
Viṣṇudharmottara, Baroda Oriental Series.
Viṣvakarmaprakāśa Śrī Maheśvara, Varanasi, 1911.

INDEX

Abhaya (Mudrā), 74, 82
Ābu (Mt.) , 66
Āditi, 19
Āditya, 12, 19, 20, 21, 25, 27, 32, 37 38, 39, 52, 60, 61, 64, 79, 82, 83, 89, 102
Āditya Bhakta, 26
Āditya Pratimā, 63
Āditya Vardhan, 102
Āditya Sen, 103
Āgamas, 52, 53
Agarvala V.S. (Dr.), 101
Agni, 19, 27, 30, 99
Ahyanga, 37
Aindra, 15
Aitareya Āranyaka, 8
Aivyaonghen, 24, 42, 100
Ajantā, 101
Akshamālā, 60
Alberuni, 24, 104, 106
Āliḍha (Posture), 85, 86
Amarakośa, 39
Aṁśa, 19
Aṁśumadbhedāgama,31, 40
Ānandagiri, 21
Ananta, 35
Anantaguphā, 101
Anuṣṭubh, 33, 37, 98
Aparājita, 15
Apollo, 16
Apratihata, 15
Apsras, 35, 36
Arab (Writers), 104
Arakan, 77
Arbhavasu, 98
Ardhshir-II, 101
Arjuna, 14, 40
Arka-Kshetra, 105
Artha, 31, 35
Arthaśastra, 14, 15
Aruṇa, 31, 33, 34, 39, 40, 45, 55, 56, 57, 58, 59, 60, 61, 62, 65, 68, 69, 70, 73, 74, 75, 77, 79, 82, 84, 85, 86, 88, 93, 97, 98, 99, 107.
Āryan, 16, 39, 102
Aryaman, 27, 38, 39
Assyro-babylonians, 16
Aṣṭādhyāyi, 13
Āśvalāyana Gṛhyasūtra, 10, 20
Aśvini (devatā), 30, 47, 48, 57, 59, 62, 63, 67
Aświns, 97
Atharvaveda, 5, 10, 27, 39, 40
Avesta, 24, 30, 45, 100
Aviyānga, 34, 57, 100
Avyanga, 24, 37, 41, 43, 46, 47, 59, 60, 63,

Bagapura, 106
Bagho, 39
Bāṇa (Poet), 101
Banḍuka, 90
Bendall, 92
Bhadrakarṇeśvara, 12
Bhaga, 19, 38, 39
Bhājā, 17, 53, 101
Bhandarkar R.G., 100
Bhāratamātā, 7
Bharatapur, 104
Bharhut, 2
Bharukacca, 25
Bhauma, 28, 30, 92
Bhavabhūti, 21
Bhīma, 12
Bhīmadeva I, 64
Bhīmanātha, 65
Bhū, 33
Bhumarā, 55
Bhuvaneśwara, 68
Bihar, 86, 94, 104
Bloch (Dr.), 85
Bodhagayā, 18, 53, 68, 101, 107
Brahmā, 34, 36, 58, 62, 63, 66, 69, 70, 73, 74, 78, 99
Brāhma, 15
Brāhmadeva, 22
Brahman, 21
Bṛhaspati, 28, 31, 72, 79, 85, 88, 92
Bṛhati, 33, 37, 98
Bṛhatsaṁhitā, 17, 23, 32, 42, 45, 46, 94, 95, 100
Buddha, 1, 2, 3

Buddha, 28, 31, 72, 79, 88, 92
Buddhist (Art), 1, 2,
Buddhist (Monument), 50, 62,
Buddhagayā, 94
Bulandsahar, 25
Burgess, 65
Burmā, 76, 77

Candra, 12, 28, 34, 79, 92
Candrabhāgā (river), 23
Caturvarga Cintāmaṇi, 37
Cālukya, 59, 61, 93, 104, 107
Chanda (Mr.), 83
Chandimuda, 104
Chāyā, 31, 32, 47, 48, 81, 84, 86, 93, 96, 97
Chidambaram, 73
Chitor, 91, 92
Chittorgarh, 104
Chitragupta, 43, 56
Chitrakarma, 14
Coomaraswamy A.K. (Dr.), 53, 79, 80
Cousen (Mr.), 64, 91, 92
Cunningham, 2, 50, 68, 106
Cutch, 101
Cuttaka, 105

Dacca, 104
Daḍavā (Saurāṣṭra), 67
Dadda-I, 25
Dadda-II, 25
Dakṣa, 19, 38
Daṇḍa, 29, 30, 31, 32, 33, 34, 35, 44, 58, 59, 60, 61, 62, 63, 65, 73, 75, 77, 81, 85, 95, 99, 101, 107
Dānakhaṇḍa, 38
Daṇḍa-nāyaka, 30, 62, 99
Daṇḍi, 30, 36, 99, 100
Daśapur, 93
Daśāvatāra (Cave), 79
Deo Baraṇārk (Inscription), 103, 127
Devaviṣṇu, 25
Dhanada, 43
Ḍhāṅk (Saurāṣṭra), 67
Dharapaṭṭa, 25
Dharma, 31, 33, 35
Dharmarāja (temple), 69
Dharmasūtra, 11
Dhātā, 43
Dhātrī, 37, 38
Dhūmāvatī, 12
Dinājpur, 104
Diṇḍi, 31
Divākara, 21
Droṇācarya, 12
Duladeo (temple), 57
Duryodhana, 14
Dvādaśādityas, 16
Dyau, 33, 96, 97
Dyāvā, 96

Earth, 99
Earth (goddess), 75, 82, 84,
Egyptian, 16, 75,
Ekalavya, 12
Elements of Hindu Iconography, 61
Ellora, 55, 56, 93
Epics, 12

Fergusson, 2
Fleet, 103
Foucher (Mr.), 1

Gaṇapati, 92
Gāndhāra (School), 2, 3, 54
Gandharvās, 36, 37, 63, 71, 82
Ganeśa, 9
Gārhapatyāgāra, 7
Gārhwa (Allahabad), 55
Garuḍa, 24, 31, 34, 98
Gaudian (Sculptures), 74, 84
Gauramukha, 24
Gautama Dharmasūtra, 11
Gāyatri, 20, 33, 37, 98, 102
Go, 96
Gop, 104
Govindapur, 24, 126
Graeco - Buddhist, 18
Greek(s), 16, 68
  Artists, 1
Grünwedel (Dr.), 1
Gudimallam, 58
Gujarat, 89, 104
Gupta, 18, 41, 55, 77, 80
Gupta Art, 80, 101
  Emperors, 102
  images, 101
Gurjar kings, 25
  Prathiar, 66
Gwalior, 25
  inscription, 103

Hackin (Mr.), 77, 101
Haṁsapura, 106
Hansi, 62
Harappa, 3
Harappan Art, 1
Harihara, 79
Harṣa, 101
Harṣavardhan, 21, 103
Helios, 16
Hema Candra, 39
Hemādri, 43
Heti, 37
Hindu Mythology, 92
Hiraṇya, 104
Hiraṇya-Pāṇi, 5
Holi-festival, 23
Hoyaṣalā, 59, 60, 61, 107
Huṇa, 25
Huṇa-Toramāna, 25
Harikeśa, 98

Icons, 44
Indo-Āryans, 16, 51
Indo-Europeans, 16
Indo-Iranians, 16, 19
Indore, 25
Indore Copper plate, 102
Indo-Scytheans, 25
Indra, 19, 34, 39
Indus Valley, 3
Iranian, 16, 40, 41, 42, 48, 54, 78
Iśvara, 22

Jagannātha Puri, 105
Jagati, 33, 36, 37, 98
Jamadgni, 46
Jambuvati, 23
Jaraśabda, 24
Jaraśasta, 24
Jayanta, 15
Jivita gupta II, 103
Junāgaḍha, 67, 93
Jupiter, 72, 79, 85, 88, 92, 99

Kabul, 101
Kadvār (Somanātha), 66
Kaegi, 6
Kailāsa (Ellora), 78, 93
Kalchuris, 104
Kālidāsa, 54
Kālikā, 12
Kāma, 34, 35
Kāmākhyā, 12
Kamaṇḍalu, 60
Kanauj, 26
Kañcuka, 39, 40
Kandahar, 104
Kaṇḍolā (hill), 90
Kaniṣka, 41
Kāntimaṇḍala, 31, 59
Kapaḍvanj, 68
Kapila Saṁhitā, 105
Karaṇḍa makuṭa, 31
Karnāṭadeśa, 61, 107
Karṇa, 46
Kārtikeya, 30
Kārvan, 64
Kashmir, 104, 106
Kaśyapa, 9, 13
Kaśyapapura, 106
Kāṭhaka Saṁhitā, 5
Kāṭhiawāḍa, 89, 92, 104
Kāṭhis, 90
Kauṣika Sūtra, 9
Kauśitaki, 20
Kauṭilya, 14
Kavaca, 39, 40, 42, 43, 46, 47
Kavacin, 40, 43
Kavasa 40
Kāveri-Pākkam, 56
Keśava, 34
Ketu, 28, 31, 72, 79, 88, 92
Khadir, 20
Khair khaneh, 77, 101
Khajuraho, 56, 57
Khaṭvānga, 62
Khmèr (Art), 75, 76
Khurāsa (Village), 93
Khuśru, 101
Khiching (Orissa), 104
Kinderkheda, 104
Kinnara, 81
Kinnari, 82
Kiriṭa, 32, 39, 40, 41, 57, 61, 62, 67, 81, 82, 83, 107, 108,
Kiriṭin, 39, 40
Kiriṭamukuṭa, 58, 63, 82, 83
Kīrtimukha, 58, 69, 71, 80, 83
Konāraka, 62, 69, 70, 84, 85, 103, 104, 105
Kratusthalā, 37
Kṛṣṇa, 23, 25, 28, 90, 102, 105

Kubera, 31, 34, 43
Kulah Cap, 54, 101
Kumāra gupta, 102
Kuṁbhāravādā, 56
Kuṇḍalas, 31, 32, 46, 57, 63, 65, 67, 73, 74, 80, 82
Kuṇḍi, 43
Kunti, 46
Kuṣāṇa, 41, 42, 54, 55, 80, 101
Kusti, 24
Kutch, 25

Lākhā phulāni, 90
Lakṣmī, 90
Limboji Mātā (Delmal), 66
Linga, 34
Linga rāja (temple), 68

Macdonell (Prof.), 98
Madirāgṛham, 15
Madurā, 105
Magas, 23, 24, 34
Magian, 24, 101
Magi, 23, 24
Mahābhārata, 12, 45, 46, 98
Mahābhāṣya, 12, 13
Mahārāṣṭra, 61
Maheśa, 66
Maheśvara, 73, 74
Maitraka, 25, 104
Maitreya, 37
Majumdar R.C., 19
Makaradhvaja, 29
Mālatimādhava, 21
Manda, 104
Mandasor, 24, 93, 102, 123
Maṅgala, 79, 87, 88, 92
Manu, 10, 11, 33, 97
Manyu, 20
Manuypati, 20
Marduk, 16
Mārtaṇḍa, 19, 104
Mars, 72, 79, 87, 92, 99
Mathura, 105, 107
Mauryas, 14
Mayūra (Poet), 21
Mayūra bhanja, 28
Mayūra śataka, 21
Mercury, 79, 88, 92
Melcheri, 56
Mihira Gotra, 24
Mihirakula, 25, 103
Mihira (Worship), 24
Mihira Yast, 29
Mithra, 16
Mitra, 19, 20, 27, 28, 29, 38, 39
Mitra (Mr.), 72
Moḍherā, 25, 63, 92, 104
Mohenjo-daro, 3
Mokṣa, 35
Moon, 34, 58, 69, 72, 79, 88, 92, 99
Mrohaung (Akyab Dist.), 76, 77
Multan, 25, 102, 103, 104, 105, 106
Mūrtivijnāna, 73
Museums
Bangiya Sāhitya Parishad, 80
Boston, 17, 78
British, 83, 74
Calcutta (Indian Museum), 18, 56, 79, 85, 91
Junagadh, 67
Lucknow, 18
Madras, 60
Mathurā, 18, 28, 41, 54, 57, 101
Rājputānā, 18
Varendra Research Soc., 18
Watson (Rajkot), 67
Worcester (Lucknow), 18, 79, 80

Nāgas, 37
Nagendranath Vasu (Mr.), 28, 29, 30
Nagnajit, 17, 18
Nārāyaṇa, 69, 74
Narasiṁhadeva, 104
Navagrahas, 17, 27, 68, 72, 79, 80, 83, 88, 89, 91
Nikṣubhā, 24, 29, 31, 58, 59, 60, 73, 74, 96, 97
Niṣprabhā, 36

Orissa, 103, 105

Padmāsana, 57, 65, 66
Pahlava, 41
Pāla, 74, 84, 103
Pallava, 56
Pālanpur, 68
Pāṇḍu, 46
Pāṇini, 3, 12, 13, 14, 40
Pankti, 33, 37, 98
Parmāditya bhakta, 26
Parasees, 24, 39, 100

Pārsikas, 54
Paraśurāmeśvara (temple), 58
Pasthar, 104
Patañjali, 3, 12, 13, 14
Persia, 100
Persian, 54, 92, 101
Piludrā (Mehsana), 68
Piṅgala, 30, 31, 32, 33, 34, 35, 36, 43, 44, 58, 59, 60, 61, 62, 63, 65, 73, 75, 77, 81, 82, 84, 95, 99, 100, 101, 107
Pītāmbara, 39
Planets, 28, 76, 85
Prabhā, 97
Prabhākara Vardhana, 103
Prabhā maṇḍala, 41, 61, 66, 67, 108
Prabhāsa, 65, 66
Prabhāvali, 60
Pratihāra, 65
Pratyuṣā, 31, 53, 55, 56, 59, 62, 65, 75, 81
Pratyālīḍha, 85, 86
Pṛthivi, 57, 81, 82, 96, 97
Pulastya, 37
Punjab, 62, 104
Purāṇa
  Agni Purāṇa, 17, 34, 36, 44, 59
  Bhaviṣya, 23, 24, 25, 28, 30, 37, 47, 59, 62, 96, 99, 100, 105
  Brahmāṇḍa, 36
  Brahmavaivarta, 17
  Kūrma, 38, 98
  Matsya Purāṇa, 17, 35, 44, 57, 77, 94, 95, 97, 100
  Mārkaṇḍeya, 17, 38, 47, 48
  Padma, 17, 37
  Sāmba, 23, 38, 49
  Skanda, 90
  Varāha, 23, 38, 105
  Viṣṇu, 37
  Viṣṇudharmottara, 17, 32, 34, 42, 51, 100
Puruṣasūkta, 22
Pūrvakāraṇāgama, 17, 45
Puṣan, 38

Rāhu, 28, 31, 72, 79, 80, 88, 92
Rai Prasanna Kumar Pal Bahadur, 71
Raivata, 31
Rājā Māndhātā, 90
Rajasthan, 104
Rajkot, 89
Rājña, 30
Rājñī, 29, 30, 32, 33, 36, 58, 59, 60, 74, 81, 97
Rajputana, 91, 93
Rākṣas, 37, 53
Rāmāyaṇa, 12
Rander, 67
Rannādevi, 67
Ranu-pipli (Dist. Baroda), 65
Rao G. (Mr.), 40, 45, 95
Raghuvaṁśa, 54
Rathakṛta, 37
Ravi, 72, 88, 92
Revanta, 33, 46, 48, 67, 97
Rigveda, 18, 27, 40, 97, 102
Rikṣubhā, 33
Roda (Dist. Himatnagar), 65, 67
Rishis, 37
Rudra, 6, 8, 34, 35, 38
Rupamaṇḍana, 17

Sadāśiva, 58
Saḍviṁśa Brāhmaṇa, 7
Saināpatya 15
Śakas, 24, 41
Śakadvipa, 23, 24, 25, 28, 29
Śakti, 62
Samabhanga (Pose), 68, 81
Samapāda, 81, 82
Samarāngaṇa Sūtradhāra, 38
Sāmaveda, 5
Sāmba, 23, 24, 25, 102, 105
Sāmbapura, 105, 106
Saṁhitās, 4
Śānayantra, 43
Saṁjñā, 43, 47, 73, 86, 93, 97
Śanaiścara, 88
Sanchi, 2
Sandhyā, 97
Śani, 28, 30, 72, 79, 92, 97
Sanjadvasu, 98
Śankara, 21
Śankhakarṇeśvara, 12
Sānkhyāyana Brāhmaṇa, 8
Santoshi Mā, 7
Sapta Samudri, 54
Śārdā tilaka, 36
Sarkhej (Dist. Ahmedabad), 67
Saraṇyu, 48
Saraswati, 72
Sassanian, 54, 77, 101

Śatapatha Brāhmaṇa, 19
Saturn, 34, 72, 79, 88, 92, 99
Sauras, 21, 26
Saurāṣṭra, 65
Savarṇā, 48, 58, 81
Sāvarṇi, 97
Savitar, 20
Savitṛ, 38, 39, 102
Scythians, 55, 102
Senas, 103
Sendrakas, 104
Shahpur-II, 101
Shahpur-III, 101
Siddhapur, 68
Śilāditya-I, 25
Śilparatna, 32
Śilpaśāstra, 4, 18, 97
Śirin (Queen), 10
Śirobandha, 81, 82
Śirohi, 104
Śiva, 12, 14, 15, 30, 34, 56, 57, 58, 62, 74, 78, 89, 92
Śivabhāgavata, 13
Skanda, 12, 14, 29, 30, 99
Skandagupta, 102
Smārta books, 10, 11
Smṛti (text), 21
Soma, 30, 72, 83, 88, 92
Somanātha, 65, 66, 104
Somanātha (Pāṭaṇa), 89
Spooner (Dr.), 50
Sraoshavarez, 30
Śrauṣa, 30
Śrauta Sūtra, 9
Śrī (goddess), 2
Śrī Viśvakarmāvatāra śāstra, 17, 45
Sten Konow (Dr.), 2
Stirling (Mr.), 72
Subrahmaṇya, 21
Sujātkhān, 90
Sujihva, 23
Śukra, 28, 31, 34, 72, 79, 88, 92
Śula, 33
Sun, 16, 17, 20, 21, 22, 23, 24, 25, 26, 27, 28, 30, 32, 33, 34, 35, 36, 37, 39, 41, 42, 44, 45, 46, 47, 48, 49, 50, 51, 52, 53, 54 56, 57, 62, 63, 67, 69, 72, 76, 77, 78, 79, 86, 88, 89, 90, 91, 93, 95, 97, 98, 100, 102, 103, 104, 105, 107
  God, 6, 16, 17, 22, 23, 26, 28, 29, 31, 33, 34, 39, 40, 41, 42, 43, 44, 45, 46, 48, 49, 51, 52, 54, 55, 56, 57, 58, 59, 61, 62, 63, 65, 67, 68, 69, 70, 71, 72, 73, 77, 78, 79, 81, 84, 89, 92, 94, 95, 96, 97, 98, 99, 100, 101, 102, 103, 106
Suprabhedāgama, 31, 40
Sureṇu, 97
Sureśvara, 55, 56
Sūrya, 16, 17, 19, 21, 22, 25, 27 28, 30, 31, 32, 34, 35, 36, 37, 38, 39, 40, 41, 42, 43, 44, 45, 46, 47, 52, 53, 54, 55, 56, 57, 58, 59, 60, 61, 62, 63, 64, 65, 66, 67, 68, 69, 70, 73, 74, 75, 76, 77, 78, 79, 80, 82, 83, 84, 85, 86, 87, 88, 89, 90, 91, 92, 94, 96, 97, 98, 100, 101, 104, 107, 108
  Maṇḍala, 29
  Nārāyaṇa, 22, 65, 66, 69
  ratha, 36
  śataka, 21
Sūriyanārkoyil, 89
Sūryopaniṣad, 37
Suṣumṇā, 98, 99
Sūtrapādā, 89, 104
Sureśvara 56
Suvarcalā, 33
Suvarcasā, 32, 58, 81, 97
Suvarṇā, 32, 84
Swaraka, 98

Tamil nāḍu, 58, 60
Tanjore (District), 89
Tantras, 52
Tapti, 97
Tārkṣya, 44
Tarṇetara, 90
Thān, 87, 90, 91, 104
Tilaka mark, 81
Taittirīya Āraṇyaka, 8,9
Taittrīya Saṁhita, 5
Traipuraṣadeva (temple), 89
Trimūrti, 66, 73
Trinetreśvara (temple), 90
Triṣṭubh, 33, 36, 98
Triśulapāṇi, 12
Tusa, 104
Tvaṣṭā, 8, 9
Tvaṣṭṛ, 38, 47, 49
Twaṣṭrā, 97

Udarabandha, 41, 60, 61, 63, 74, 107
Udayācala, 105
Udayagiri, 2, 95
Udīcya, 34, 43, 100
Udīcya veśa, 39, 41, 42, 45, 46, 47, 95, 101
Ugrasena, 24
Unza, 65, 66
Upanayana, 20
Upaniṣada, 3
Uṣā, 83, 86, 88, 96, 97, 98
Uṣṇik, 33, 98
Uṣṇis, 37
Uttarakuru, 47

Vaḍnagar, 68
Vaijayanta, 15
Vaiśravaṇa, 15
Vaiṣṇavism and Śaivism, 100
Vaivasvata, 97
Vājal deva, 89
Vāja Saneyi Saṁhitā, 4
Valabhi, 25
Valaya, 82
Vāmana, 12
Varada (Mudrā), 74
Varāha (temple), 66
Varāhamihira, 17, 18, 23, 45, 100
Vārcha, 29
Vardhan (Emperor), 103
Varmans, 103
Varuṇa, 5, 19, 20, 27, 34, 38, 79
Vaṣiṣthāśrama, 66
Vāsudeva, 12, 34, 35
Vāsuki, 37
Vāta, 19
Vāyu, 19
Vedas, 4, 102
Vedic Age, 1
Vedic Mythology, 79, 98
Vedic texts, 22
Venus, 72, 79, 88, 92, 99
Vidhātā, 100
Vināyaka, 9, 31
Vinatā, 34
Viśākha, 14
Viśāladeva (Thakur), 89
Viśālākṣi, 89
Visavada, 104
Viṣṇu, 9, 12, 14, 17, 21, 28, 37, 38, 39, 40, 49, 52, 58, 63, 65, 66, 69, 70, 73, 74, 89, 92, 98
Viśvakarmā, 8, 43, 44, 47, 48, 94, 96, 98
Viśvakarman, 57
Viśvakarmā (Śilpa), 29
Viśvakarmaśāstra, 17, 38, 44, 83
Viśveśvara, 89
Viśwaśraba, 98
Vivasvān, 38, 48
Viyānga, 34, 42, 100
Vogel, 54,
Vratakhaṇḍa, 43

Waḍhawāṇa, 89
Wāloji, 90
Wāsuki, 90
Wilkin, 92
Wuntitaung, 77

Yajñopavīta, 31, 57, 62, 65
Yajurveda (White), 4
Yakṣas, 37
Yama, 9, 29, 30, 32, 33, 34, 38, 97, 99
Yami, 97
Yāmya, 15
Yāska, 19
Yāviyānga, 32, 33, 34, 43
Yuan-chwang, 103, 106
Yudhiṣṭhira, 20

Zend Avesta, 29
Zarathushtra, 24, 28
Zoroastrian, 42, 50

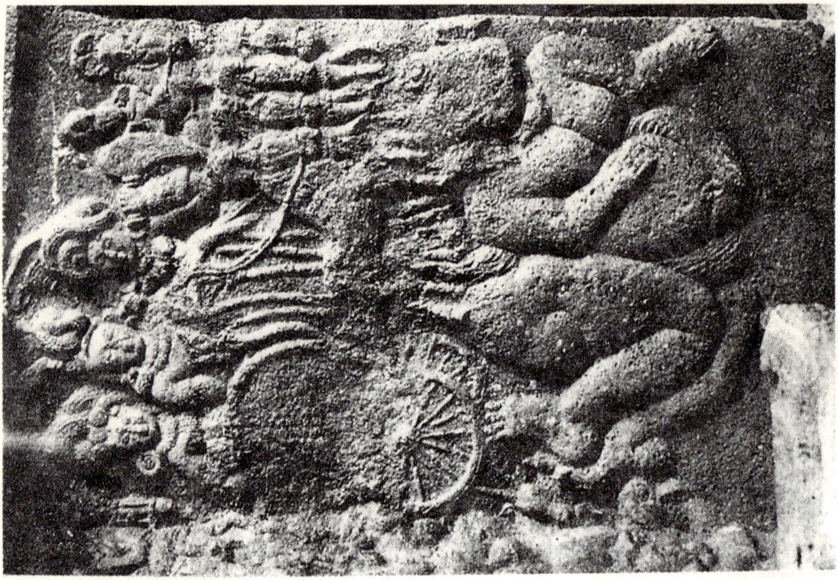

Fig.2 Sūrya – Bhājā

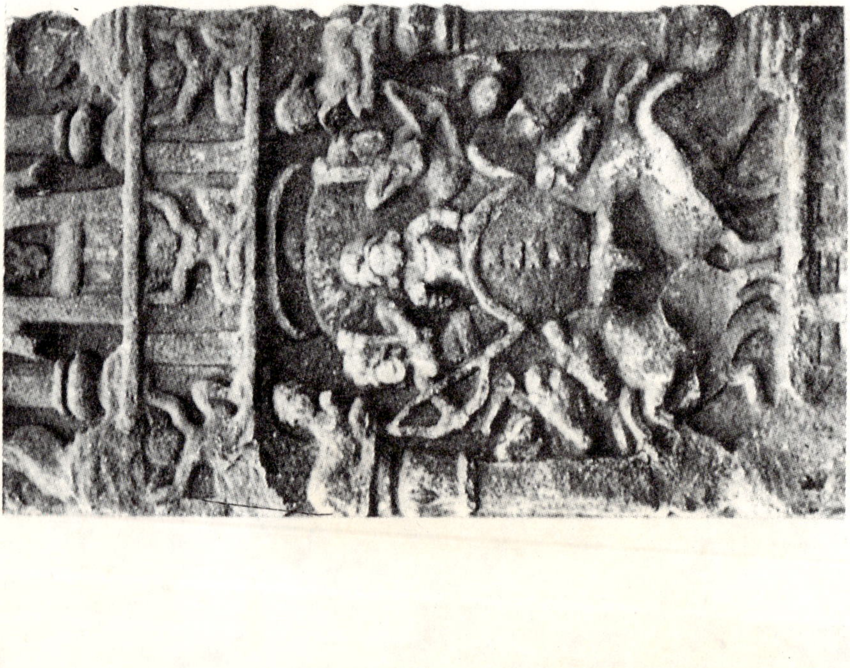

Fig.1 Sūrya – Bodhgaya Railing

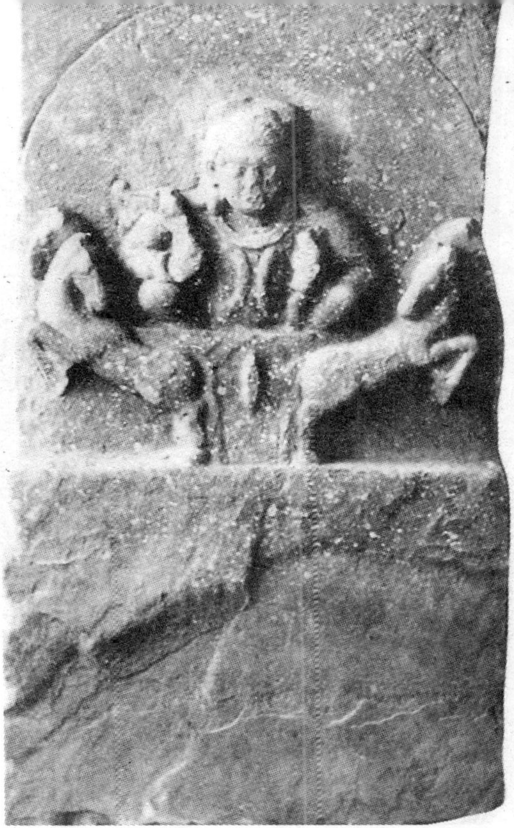

Fig.3 Sūrya – Mathura
(description on p.54)

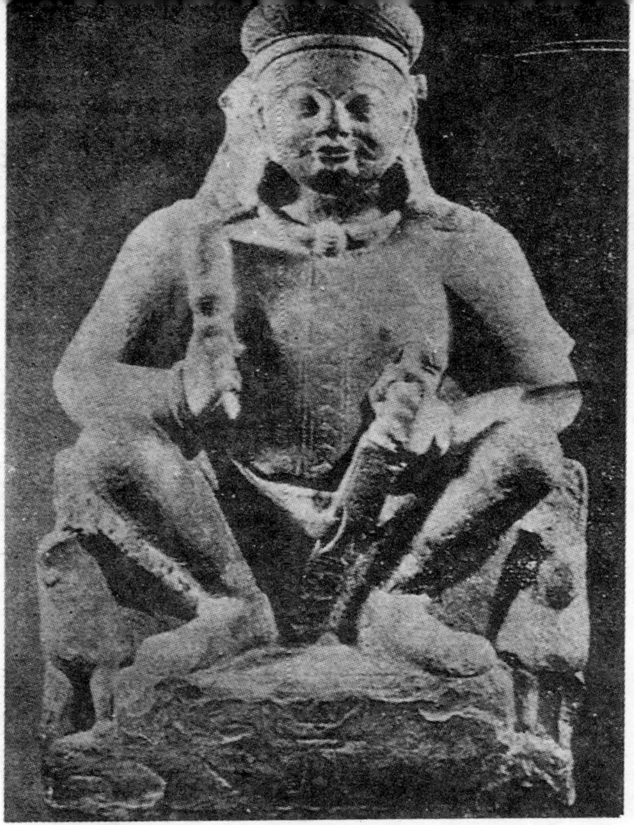

Fig.4 Sūrya (Kuṣāṇa) – Mathura
(description on p.54)

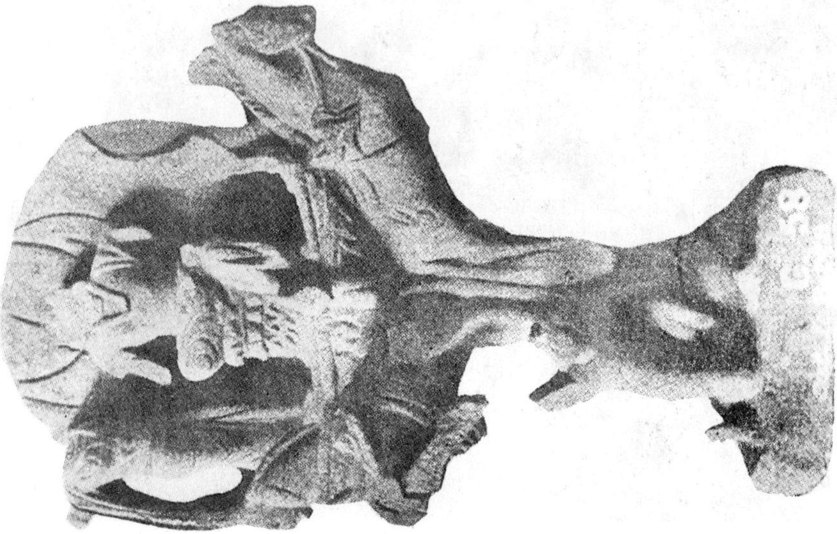

Fig.5 Sūrya – Gāndhāra
(description on p.55)

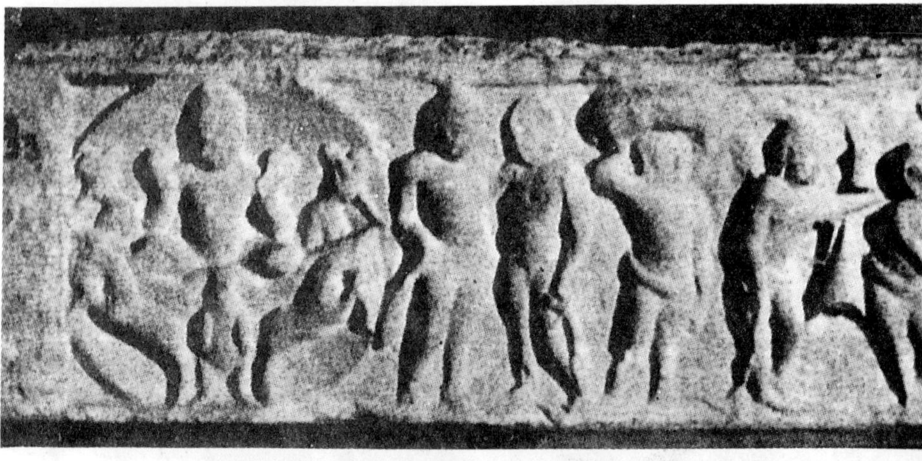

Fig.6 Sūrya – Garhwa, Allahabad (Gupta Period)
(description on p.55)

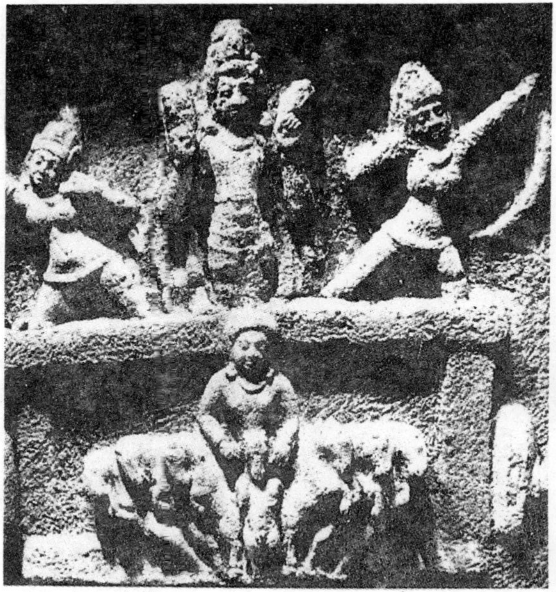

Fig.7 Sūrya – Ellora
(description on p.55)

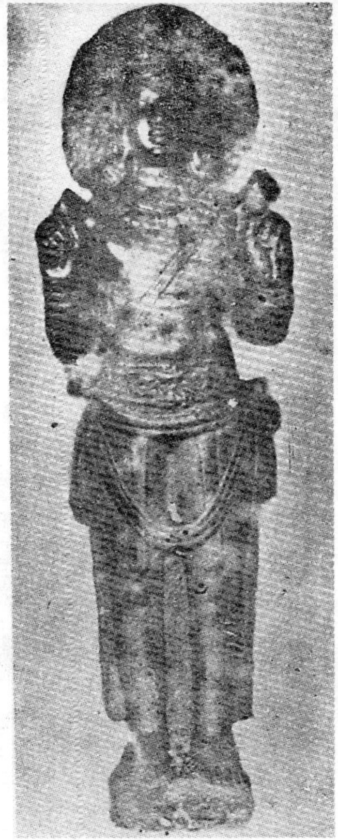

Fig.8 Sūrya – Gudimallam
(description on p.58)

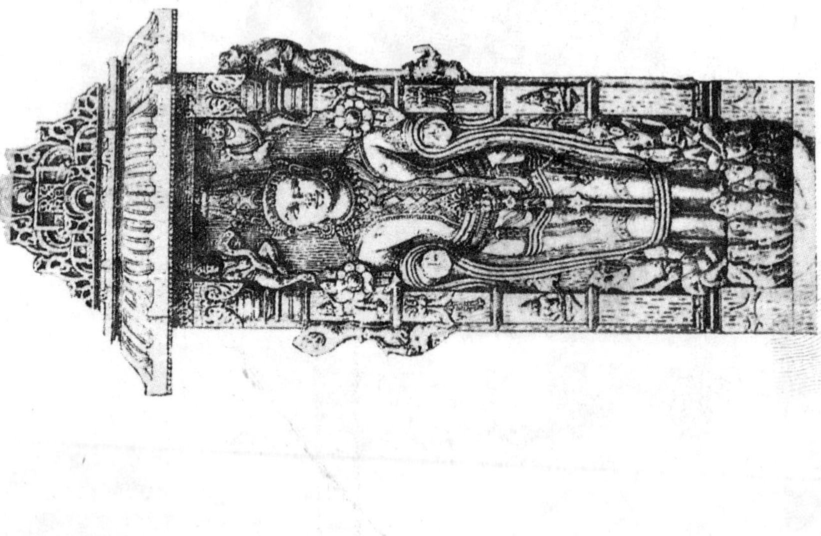

Fig.9 Sūrya – Modhera

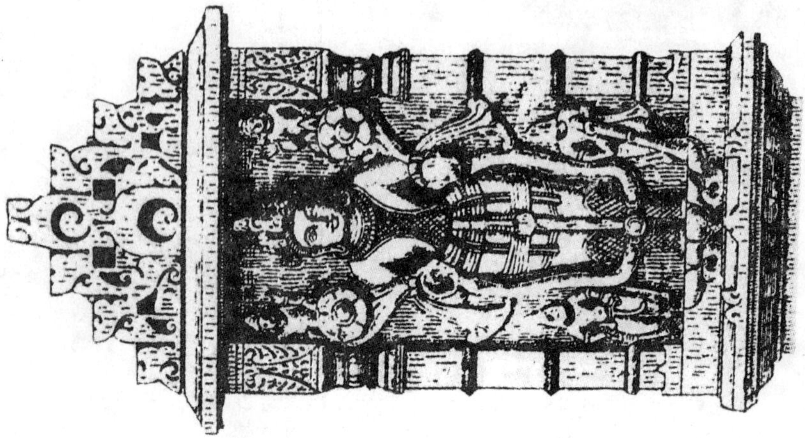

Fig.10 Sūrya – Modhera

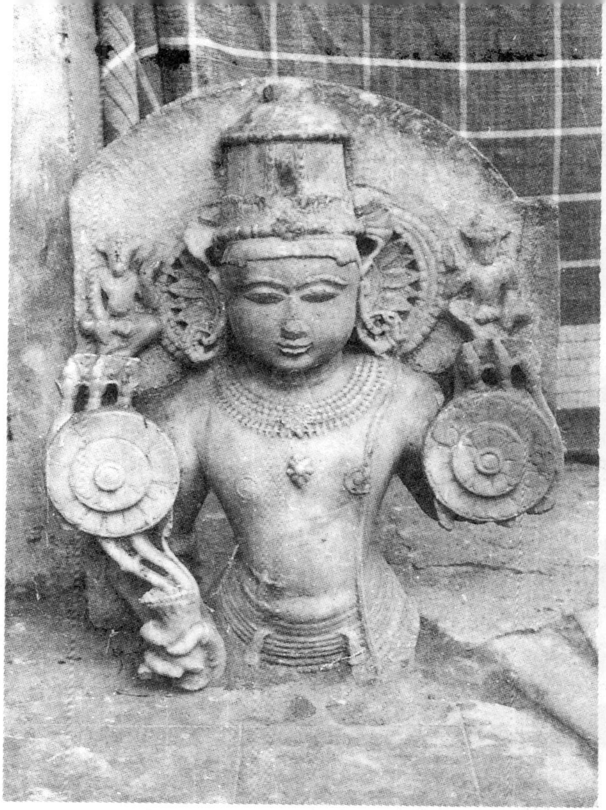

Fig.11 Sūrya – Sarkhej (Ahmedabad)
(description on p.67)

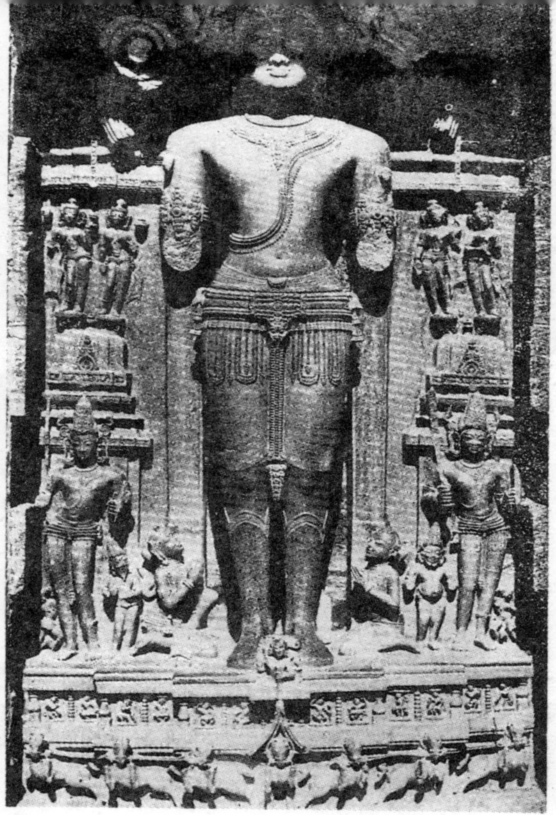

Fig.12 Sūrya – Konarka
(description on p.70)

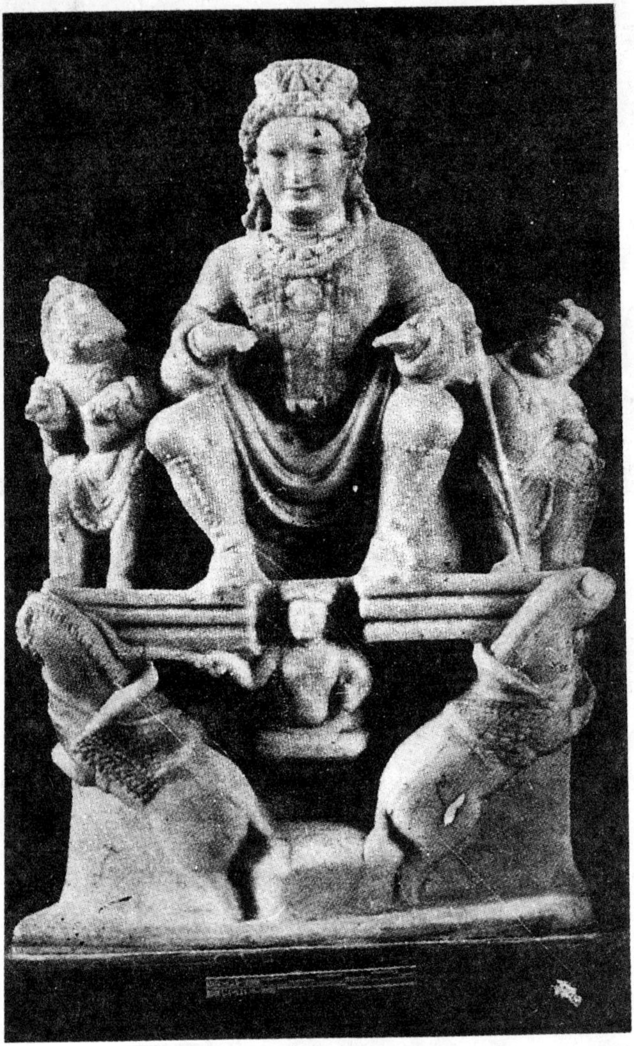

Fig.13 Sūrya – Khair Khaneh
(description on p.77)